Also by Robertson Work

Book author
*A Compassionate Civilization: The Urgency of
Sustainable Development and Mindful Activism –
Reflections and Recommendations*

General editor and contributor
Participatory Local Governance
Pro-Poor Urban Governance: Lessons from LIFE 1992-2005

Chapter Author
Changing Lives, Changing Societies
Decentralization and Power-Shift
Engaging Civil Society
Life Lessons for Loving the Way You Live
(Chicken Soup for the Soul)
New Regional Development Paradigms: Vol. 3
Reinventing Government for the 21ˢᵗ Century

Contributor
Cities, People and Poverty: UNDP Urban Strategy
Re-conceptualizing Governance
The Urban Environment

Serving People & Planet

In Mystery, Love and Gratitude

Robertson Work

ISBN: 978-1-6847-1616-6 (sc)
ISBN: 978-1-6847-1615-9 (e)

Library of Congress Control Number: 2019920210

Lulu Publishing Services rev. date: 01/06/2020

627 Davis Dr. #300
Morrisville, North Carolina,
27560 US

ADVANCE PRAISE FOR SERVING PEOPLE & PLANET: IN MYSTERY, LOVE AND GRATITUDE

"In this book, Rob Work has narrated a fascinating story of his life, demonstrating his passion for humanity and the planet, and contribution to community and leadership development through the nonprofit Institute of Cultural Affairs, United Nations Development Program and the NYU Wagner Graduate School of Public Service. The book will inspire younger generations to engage as advocates, activists, trainers and community organizers to make a difference in improving human conditions."

- G. Shabbir Cheema, PhD, senior fellow, Harvard Kennedy School; former director of UNDP Management Development and Governance Division

"What a remarkable life! You show readers who might feel despair that it is possible to change the world. I think you also do an important service by introducing us to countless individuals in vibrant organizational communities who are out there every day fearlessly working to make change. It's an eye opener for those who think the totality of our political and institutional efforts are manifested in current governments—or who think we have entered a particularly cynical, negative and disruptive era. You show that transformation is always blooming, under the surface and behind the scenes. . . . I loved the first part about your personal youthful journey and your spiritual awakening. . . . . I thought the chapters on your international assignments were the best of the book. You really captured the struggles and rewards of global citizenry, and your stories are delightful. . . . I also enjoyed your personal family journey and observed the ways that your openness to different practices and points of view inspired so much good work. This again is important for people who feel locked into ideologies and practices, and don't know how to embrace globality and diversity. . . . You are a person who has answered every call, and that vibrant message resonates throughout the book. I think the question 'What does it mean to be called . . . and answer the call' has relevance to people of all ages."

  - Catherine Whitney, nonfiction author of 50-plus books, including several best sellers

"Robertson Work's autobiography is an example of what it means to be a global citizen with heart—heart for his family and heart for all humanity. His life purpose has been lived across the world—a servant of goodness—a rarity in our current world."

  - Nancy Roof, PhD, founder of Kosmos Journal

"Have you ever wondered what is it all for, what should be done about it, and what is your role—especially in relation to such daunting global challenges as those faced by humanity today? This is the inspiring story of one "useful man", who has found answers in the very asking of such questions—every day of a long life, rich in global service and facilitative leadership. It is largely a love story—of Rob's love of the earth, his fellow earthlings and of life itself—but not without drama, tragedy and comedy as well. May you draw courage and inspiration from it, as I and many others have done so from Rob's "doing, knowing and being" over many years—to live your own life in such freedom and responsibility at this most critical time for us all and our planet."

- Martin Gilbraith, London UK, certified professional facilitator, trainer & consultant; International Association of Facilitators (IAF), chair 2011-12; and ICA International, president 2013-16

"Rob writes as he lives—with integrity, passion and compassion—as he says yes again and again to his assignments in every season. I highly recommend this book to anyone who wants to be aligned to calling, who is searching for meaning, who is responding to a life of service to humankind and care of the Earth in all its messy splendor. Reading this book is like being held in a warm embrace, as we journey with this man in every turn of page, experiencing all his adventures around the world and diving deep into his reflections on identity, family, love, life, loss and purpose. I am honored to endorse this book and to call Rob my friend and mentor."

- Lowie Rosales Kawasaki, former United Nations Habitat program officer, Nairobi

"At the heart of Rob's life has been a 'blessed unrest' that for 75 years he has kept reflecting and acting upon two key questions: 'What is humanness?' and 'How do I be of service?' It has been an honor to work with Robertson Work for the last 43 years; he lives every day with love in his heart. He attracts people, funding resources, and creative ideas to the possibility he sees. Rob has made his whole life a vehicle of learning about becoming a planetary human. Join with him on this adventure of shaping possibility at this amazing time in human history. Rob has brought a new state of mind, grounded in his commitment to service, to bear on a wide variety of fields: environment, HIV and AIDS, decentralized governance, and local leadership."

- Jan Sanders, founder/director, PeoplEnergy, Canada

"Robertson Work's autobiography is a vivid example of his 75 years of life journey in which he takes us on the ups and downs of his life. They are such emotional and touching experiences that we can also experience them while going through this masterpiece. It is a must-read autobiography for all of us to realize the compassionate life and virtues of noble humanity."

- Tatwa P. Timsina, PhD, professor, Tribhuvan University; author; founding chair, ICA Nepal; and former president of ICA International

"We celebrate Rob Work's life of service. He writes of his mythic journey from growing up, a small-town boy, in Oklahoma, then as an adult working in rural villages in forsaken areas of the world and finally to the United Nations, where he was able to influence the governance of thousands of communities in the world."

- Joy Jinks, MSW, author of *Dynamic Aging;* community organizer

"Grateful to read this wonderful book, which documents 75 years of living with poor people and serving many countries. I give personal deep appreciation for Mr. Robertson Work and Mrs. Mary Work who made a life together with me possible at Kuh Du I Ri human development project in Korea."

- Rev. Dr. Park Si Won, former pastor of Bo Moon Methodist Church and director of ICA Korea

DEDICATION

This book is dedicated to my maternal great-aunt
Mary Yates Dodd
who challenged me as a boy to "be a useful man" and
to my two sons,
Benjamin Kang Work and **Christopher Edward Work**
two good men of whom I am so proud.

It is also dedicated to those in 1945 who founded the United Nations, those in the 1960s who began to create a more just and peaceful world, and in 2019 to Representative Alexandria Ocasio-Cortez, and Greta Thunberg, contemporary heroines for justice and sustainability.

"*The purpose of life is not to be happy. It is to be useful, to be honorable, to be compassionate, to have it make some difference that you have lived and lived well.*"
-Ralph Waldo Emerson

"*If you want others to be happy, practice compassion. If you want to be happy, practice compassion.*"
- His Holiness the 14th Dalai Lama

"*Why am I so happy? Because the Earth is round!*"
- Pierre Teilhard de Chardin

CONTENTS

PROLOGUE

Well, here you are. Welcome! I hope all is well with you and yours. What brings you here? What are your interests or concerns? How might reading this book be of interest to you or provide any help to you? You may know me or about me, or you may not. It's all good. Or you may simply want to visit someone else's life. If you find any of the following engaging, you may have come to the right place: community development, Oklahoma, falling in love, planet Earth, ICA, teaching, the United Nations, how to deal with the death of a loved one, dancing, how to be happy, how to be compassionate, Nepal, being a reflective being, vocation, leadership, facilitation, NYU, nonprofits, being male, travel, villages, cities, South Korea, music, food, grandchildren—many of these, none, some?

You are now reading my life as a book. This is obviously not my life. It is a book about my life. My actual life was/is much more interesting, dense, visceral, ambiguous, and multidimensional than these few words on these few pages. This book contains facts about my life and my work, descriptions, explanations, and stories based on memories, perceptions, perspectives, reflections, and analysis. This is a legacy autobiography—"auto" is the self; "bio" is life; and "graphy" is writing—a writing by the self about the life of the self. A "legacy" is a personal gift handed down from an ancestor. This book is, therefore, a gift to people and planet of the story of my work and life written by me.

I crafted this book for you as a vehicle of conveyance of my values, history, stories, accomplishments, struggles, dreams, and advice. I want to provide a report, an accounting of my living and working as I stand before my sister and fellow humans as well as before the entire Earth community of living beings and ecosystems. These printed words set in motion a dialogue between your mind and mine, between your life and mine.

I completed and published this book in 2019 for two primary reasons. One, I am deeply concerned, as are many people, probably you as well, about the multiple crises that humanity and life on Earth are currently facing, including climate chaos and ecosystem collapse, patriarchy and misogyny, fascist plutocracy and corporatocracy, systemic poverty and social deprivation, racism and xenophobia, and perpetual warfare and a culture of violence. As fellow and sister Earthlings, we are aware that life on Earth including human civilization may be in danger of collapse due to climate chaos and ecological destruction. It is, therefore, time to radically increase our love of people and planet or we may lose our species and much of life on Earth. We are beginning the critical decade of 2020 – 2030 and must mitigate and adapt to climate chaos and achieve the seventeen UN sustainable development goals (SDGs.) And two, I am now seventy-five and wanted to do this while I am still able. Therefore, I chose to share my life story as a message of hope, motivation, and maybe even some guidance for confronting and responding to these and other crises. We can individually and together face the unknown—the mystery—and empowered by love and with gratitude for the Earth community, do what is needed to change individual mindsets and behaviors and collective cultures and systems. It is possible to awaken from our trance of separation and greed and to create a compassionate-ecological civilization. Anything less will most likely be too little to save us.

I created this book in stages. First, in 1991 in Venezuela, when I was forty-five, I wrote the first draft of an introduction and Parts I and II. Then in 1994 in New York City, at fifty, I wrote the beginning of Part III. Finally, in 2019 in North Carolina, at seventy-five, I wrote the rest of Part III, as well as Parts IV, V, front and back pieces, and edited the whole manuscript before sending it to the publisher for editing and design. In order to complete the book, I reviewed my fifty-two years of journals (65 handwritten books and 192 computer-written monthly reflections-in-action), fifteen photo albums, some letters, institutional reports and artifacts, and discussed the manuscript with family and friends. Overall, this process has been a kind of spiritual retreat providing me with many new insights, patterns, questions, reflections, and decisions. Gratitude.

Part I of the book contains short chapters on my ancestry and birth, childhood, adolescence, education in high school, university, and graduate school, and initial awakening and calling. In Part II, there are chapters about my life and work in five countries when I was with a nonprofit service organization living and working in poor villages and slums. Part III has chapters concerning my time as an international civil servant providing policy advice to cities and countries on decentralized governance. In Part IV, the chapters deal with my teaching innovative leadership in graduate school, being a consultant and trainer, speaking at international conferences, blogging, and writing *A Compassionate Civilization (ACC)*. In the fifth and final part of the story, the two chapters focus on publishing the book and promoting key messages of *ACC*, engaging as a climate/justice activist, and envisioning some of my future life and work. In Parts II through V, in addition to work-related matters, there are personal and family episodes scattered throughout. The Epilogue provides my summary reflections on temporal turning points and several thematic areas of importance to me, In the Postscript, I pose a few questions to enable the reader's own reflections on the book, my life, and your life. Appendix One contains URLs of videos of some of my recent public talks, radio interviews, my blog posts and social media pages, and interviews and excerpts on other websites, along with several of my publications. Appendix Two is the revised 1991 Introduction. In the Bibliography, the reader can find other books and online resources related to my work and life.

After writing the manuscript, I brainstormed over 150 book titles. I settled on one, and then another, talked with Bonnie, my wife, and asked my social media friends to weigh in on the selection. Eventually, I came to rest on *Serving People & Planet: In Mystery, Love and Gratitude.* The title indicates what I am doing by writing this story. It is my accountability for my life and service. I stand and account for being given the gift of life and for giving my life in return as a gift. What have I done in this life for people and planet, for humanity and nature, for the Earth community in all its overwhelming beauty and tragedy? I am accounting for my life and work in the gaze of over seven billion of us humans, all animals, all plants, all the waters, the air, all minerals, all the soil, all the energy and light from our sun-star, and all the debris of colliding asteroids over the eons.

Regarding the subtitle, sometimes I feel that all I truly understand in life are these three realities. First, life is a mystery. Where do we come from? Why are we here? What is the meaning of life? Why do things happen as they do? Why is there suffering? Why is there anything rather than nothing? Where are we headed? What are we doing circling a star that encircles a galactic black hole in a universe of trillions of stars? Sheer mystery. The unknown unknown. Again and again, I have learned to trust the unknown, to trust the mystery. Second, there is love. Nothing else really makes sense to me. The Earth community first loved me and each of us as its beloved children. Without identifying with others, cherishing others, caring, loving, relieving the suffering of others and ourselves, making others happy, there is truly no other meaning or purpose to living. Why do we love? Because we are made to love. We are here to love. We are driven by love. We are called by love. And third, when all is said and done, I return to gratitude for it all, for each moment, for each event, for each being, for each struggle, for the undeserved gift of my life.

I chose an Earth-sunflower image for the book cover rather than my photo for three reasons. First, because the self is not a separate, unchanging entity limited to this skin bag and ego but is made up of all that is not the self, I wanted the cover image to be my family portrait. All of me and all of us are present in this image. This autobiography is my perception of who "I" have been and what I have done as presented from my perspective and from my memory and with my ideas and words. Yet, "my" words and perspectives are given to me by shared cultural contexts and forms, and my memories are shaped by other people, photographs, and historical contexts. And in fact, there is no "me" apart from the myriad other people, beings, things, and concepts in the story. The second reason is that the Earth and sunflowers are two of my very favorite realities and images. This picture is a sacred portrait of all life, all stories, all ideas, all of history, all of our planet's evolution, and all sentient beings present, past, and future. It is me, and I am it. We are all Earthlings and we are all sunflowers. And third, the image of an Earth-sunflower is a gift from my eleven-year-old grandson, who drew it on my seventy-fifth birthday card. Thank you, Phoenix Orion Work!

Birthday card from my grandson

If you read from beginning to end, you will, of course, experience the unfolding of a life, stage by state, chapter by chapter, year by year. Or, if you wish, you can move in and out of parts, chapters, or sections that capture your interest. As you do, think of your own life. Question mine. Why did he do that? Not do this? Dialogue with me and others in my life. What are you experiencing? Feeling? Learning? Deciding? Write about it. Talk with someone about it. Or write me your thoughts and questions.

So, welcome to a journey of serving people and planet in mystery, love, and gratitude. I am happy and honored to go with you.

o 31 July 2019, Swannanoa, North Carolina

PART ONE

EMERGING AS A VOCATED EARTHLING

Being born, growing up, learning, being called: 1944 – 1968: 0 to 24 in Texas, Oklahoma, Indiana, Illinois

In 1944, World War II was underway, The D-Day invasion took place in June. FDR announced his Economic Bill of Rights that year, then died the next year before it could be enacted. And Gandhi was freed from jail.

> *"There is a vitality, a life force, an energy, a quickening that is translated through you into action, and because there is only one of you in all of time, this expression is unique. And if you block it, it will never exist through any other medium and it will be lost. The world will not have it. It is not your business to determine how good it is nor how valuable nor how it compares with other expressions. It is your business to keep it yours clearly and directly, to keep the channel open."*
> - Martha Graham

1

A BEGINNING:
Houston, Texas

So, for the sake of brevity and humility, this story begins in 1944, the Year of the Monkey, the year of my birth, or so I was told.

I was born in Houston, Texas, United States of America, in St. Joseph's Catholic Hospital. My father was a lieutenant in the Army Air Corps, training navigators, stationed along with my mother in Houston at Ellington Field. That hot summer night my dad was on duty as officer of the day. There had been some trouble, and he was late getting to bed. A friend called him at midnight and said that they were taking his wife to the hospital. When he was relieved of duty, he drove to the hospital and was told that they had a son and that his wife was fine. He gave thanks to God. I was born on the 31st day of July, under the sign of Leo, at 8 pounds, 4 1/2 ounces, 21 inches. My parents—Moorman Robertson Work Sr., and Mary Elizabeth Duncan Work—were white, middle-class people, raised in Oklahoma in Christian homes—good, caring, sincere people. They had fallen in love and married in Durant, Oklahoma, the previous year. I can't remember anything of these early days. They come to me by virtue of photographs and parental stories, which I have come to believe and which constitute a fragment of my sense of identity.

Mother and Dad with baby Rob

My parents named me Moorman Robertson Work Jr. They had planned for nine months to name me Duncan, but then dad's mother told my mother that she would name her first-born son after his father even if his name were Methuselah! Mother was afraid that she would be sorry if she didn't; and she was so glad that she did. Dad had said all along that he didn't want a "Jr." and to put his heavy name on me. But after they named me, dad was so proud. All three of my names are Scottish family names: Moorman, man of the Scottish moor; Robertson, son of Robert; and Work, a Scottish family name from the Orkney Islands. My dad was named after his maternal uncle Dr. Moorman Robertson, who had been a medical missionary in South Korea and died in a car accident in New York City. My parents called me Rob and dad Robbie.

I was not born with a silver spoon in my mouth, but I was privileged nonetheless, not better than, just privileged: a healthy body and brain, male, white, middle class, American, a loving mother and father who went to college. Why was this my fate?

I had nothing to do with it. It was given. I showed up in this situation with these conditions and attributes. But why? For what? Martin Heidegger called it "thrownness." Accidents of birth. Accidents or destiny? Opportunities, not closed doors. An enabling environment, not a dangerous one. Not a refugee. Not destitute. Also, not the child of billionaires or royalty. Just this one. But why? There is no answer. What is it to be born? To be "thrown" like dice? To show up, to unfold, to grow, to choose?

At first, I wasn't fully human. I had no ideas, no language, no speech, no worldview, no culture, no religion, no self-control, no agency. I was a baby animal with the potentiality to become human, if cared for, fed, loved, educated, guided, and given opportunities. Without all of that and more, I would die and never realize my humanity. My mother and dad were on the front line of crafting this little one into a self, a mind, a heart, a force in society. And beyond the two of them, it would take many others to help fashion this little pup into a human being—family members, friends, doctors, farmers, teachers, and many more. Deep gratitude to everyone who called me forth, pushed me onward, provided a helping hand, a kind smile, a word of encouragement. My parents asked me to "be a good boy." Later, my great-aunt Mary Yates Dodd would challenge me to "be a useful man."

In this same light, I have been told stories of my ancestors—this is where the story begins to expand back into time—a mere 500 years or so. I have heard stories about my ancestors in Oklahoma, Kentucky, Arkansas, New England, England, Scotland, Ireland. "Yes, the Robertsons used to have a big house in Kentucky and Black slaves." From Henry Francis Work's 1902 account: "In 1692, John, Joseph, Henry & Alexander Work, brothers & families— Scottish nobility with a large retinue of servants, Covenanters of the Strictest—landed on the Coast of New Jersey, having left Scotland on account of religious persecution." Covenanters were those who remained steadfast in their Presbyterian beliefs and refused to take an oath to the king saying that he was the head of the church.

And from the book, *Work Family History: Twelve Generations of Works In America (1690 – 1969)*: "Confirmation of the surname Work as meaning 'makers and keepers of fortifications' is found in the history of the Work family in the Orkney Islands, that cluster of 62 islands lying six miles off the northern coast of Scotland." "The first mention of the Work family in the Orkneys has been found in the petition of Mary Work to the Pope, circa 1400, requesting to remarry after the death of her husband at sea." "The Scottish spelling of Work is Wark." DNA shows mostly from British Isles, including England, with significant amounts from Norway, Sweden and Denmark. "Your Grand Mother used to ride a horse and shoot a gun." These stories and data and others like them have become part of my identity. My ancestors were religious people. My ancestors had slaves. These I accept as part of my story.

My mother was born in Durant, Oklahoma, and my dad in Alton, Illinois. Odell Carr Duncan and Sally Ann Yates were my mother's parents. They had a son and two daughters—Odell, Laura Louise, and my mother. My dad's parents were John Henry Work Sr. and Arrie Elizabeth Robertson. They had two sons—John Henry Jr. and my dad. My dad's grandparents were Alexander Campbell Work and Sarah Jane Fisher, and Charles S. Robertson and Mary Green; my mother's grandparents, John and Rebecca Yates, and William and Amanda Duncan.

But, of course, there are a few gaps, actually gigantic gaps. Who were all of my ancestors? What about before 1400? What about in the year 2000 BC? What about a million years ago? A few gaps. Nevertheless, the stories of history (five thousand-plus years' worth) and evolution (millions and billions of years' worth) fill in the gaps in my story. I accept these larger stories as part of my story. There are also theories about reincarnation and past lives, but these have not found their way into my story as it currently exists.

Because some of my ancestors had slaves and perhaps others played a role in the genocide of native people in America, I express my regret and sorrow and commitment to some form of reparations.

2

CHILDHOOD: Okmulgee and Durant, Oklahoma

The year after my birth, the United States dropped atomic bombs on precious human beings in Japan; and in the spirit of "never again," the United Nations was born on the same day as my dad's birthday, October 24.

Well, the baby grew as babies are wont to do. At three weeks, we were back in Durant with my first photo taken with my grandmother Duncan and my mother. I stayed there while mother and dad were stationed in Lincoln, Nebraska. Soon, I joined them in Dyersburg, Tennessee, and celebrated my first birthday in Gulfport, Mississippi. When I was 2, dad left the armed service as a captain. In 1946-48, we were in Stillwater, Oklahoma, at Oklahoma A&M (now Oklahoma State University), where dad studied under the GI Bill, passed the month before I was born, and received his master's degree in business. At about 3 and 1/2 years of age, I started trying to rhyme everything and made up a long song and stories. I loved to color and draw. I printed my name "Rob" at four years old.

Our family at Theta Pond at Oklahoma A&M (now OSU)

We then moved to Okmulgee, Oklahoma, where dad taught business in college and coached sports, and I started the first grade. We lived in a little yellow house, rather near to Henryetta, where my dad's mother lived. Her husband, my grandfather, had passed away when my dad was fourteen. When I was four years old, I got a baby brother named James Duncan. He was to be my only sibling. He was a fat, cute, happy baby with blond hair. I, by that time, was growing taller and thinner, and my light brown hair was turning darker. I have always been the "big brother." This is part of my identity. I loved my little brother, and we played and wrestled for many years. We played in cardboard boxes, rode our bikes, climbed on our dad, wore our cowboy hats, went fishing, hunted Easter eggs, and dressed up as Indians and pirates.

Sometimes we visited my beloved grandmother Arrie Work in Henryetta along with my cousins, aunt and uncle. My grandmother was a wonderful lady. She told us stories about Kentucky, and was a devout Baptist. My three cousins, Johnny, Pamela (PK), and

Susan, my brother, and I loved to play together in grandmother's yard. Cousin Merrilee joined us later. Their mother, my aunt Hiahwahnah Hudson Work, was one-half Choctaw.

Other times we would visit my other beloved grandmother, Sally Duncan in Durant in southeastern Oklahoma. She was a lovely lady who lived alone in an old, white-frame house surrounded by crepe myrtle and iris. Her husband, my granddad, had also died when my mother was a girl. Grandmother Duncan was a devout Christian. In Durant, we also had cousins, aunts and uncles. My brother and I loved to play with our two first cousins, Ben and Betty, in our grandmother's big yard. We had two other first cousins, Chris and Margaret Ann, who lived in north Texas and would sometimes visit grandmother when we were there. We would play and play together. Black people couldn't live in Durant. They lived in a little town outside of Durant called Calera. That didn't seem right.

In Okmulgee, we played with other children in the neighborhood. I remember very little from this period. Most of my memories are tied to photographs and stories that my parents, brother and I rehearse. One story that has stayed with me mysteriously is about a little girl in the neighborhood. One day while we were playing, I hit her on the head with a toy. She said, "That didn't hurt at all." Then she ran home crying. Why do I remember that particular story out of all the events of that time? I was sorry for what I did and hoped that she was OK. I haven't done anything like that since. My father called me "my little tomato." Why did he call me that? What did that do to me? My brother and I were great playmates. We built forts together, played with our toy soldiers, played hide-and-seek, and many other activities.

When I was in the first grade, my teachers discovered that I could not read the blackboard and that I would need glasses. I went to the optometrist and did eye exercises. Round and round, side to side, up and down, my eyeballs would go. The optometrist said that if I didn't exercise my eyes, I might go blind. I had progressive nearsightedness. So, I began to wear bifocals at an early age. I also had what were called "buck teeth." My front teeth protruded a bit. Later, I got braces and straightened my teeth. Sometimes, I felt that many things were wrong with me and had to be fixed. I was rather shy. I parted my straight brown hair on the right side, where I had a "cowlick." I remember thinking about what difference it would make if I went to a party at someone's house or if I didn't. What would be the difference? For me? For the party'? This was a kind of mystery to me, not knowing what, if any, the difference would be.

I really don't have many memories about primary school. I sometimes think that I would like to do something that would stimulate my memory so that I could remember many things that happened to me when I was a child. My first school was named Horace Mann Elementary School. I lived very near to the school and walked. Later, when I was ten, we moved back to Durant, Oklahoma, and I went to Washington Irving Elementary School. I have a vivid memory of telling the teacher on some of the other boys who were acting up in the back of the classroom. That afternoon I was afraid that they would get me after school on my way home. But they didn't. Why do I remember that one thing? What about all of the other million things that happened to me? What was I dreaming about at this time?

3

ADOLESCENCE, AND GRANDMOTHER'S PASSING: Durant, Oklahoma

Then came junior high school. I liked Ms. Harris, my English teacher, and enjoyed shop with Mr. Dobson where we made things out of metal, wood and plastic. I still have a lacquered wooden bookshelf with embossed metal ends with images of lions (Leo) that I made along with a fluted clear plastic container. I have almost no other active memories of this time.

Duncan and I played at boxing, played baseball with dad, rode our bikes with our friends, and played basketball with our cousins.

Rev. Charles Bretz baptized me by immersion at the First Christian Church in Durant. Afterward, my family mentioned that when he dunked me backward, my feet stuck up out of the baptismal water. I had perfect attendance in Sunday school and wore my many medals on my shirt or jacket. I was taught to love my neighbor as myself.

I didn't enjoy getting my hair cut, as I worried that the barber might cut my ear or cut my hair in a wrong way. What was intriguing was looking in the mirrors in the barbershop. I could see my image looking back at me, and then reflected again and again in mirrors in front and in back of me.

Then came high school. I begin to remember more here. I took Latin. I enjoyed mathematics and writing essays. I played the French horn in the high school symphonic band, conducted by Kenneth Peters. One year we won class triple "A" in a tristate competition, even though we were from a town of 10,000 and competed against huge cities in Texas such as Corpus Christi. I enjoyed playing in the band immensely but never felt that I perfected my skill with the French horn. The conductor had told me that I had a very good sense of pitch and should play either the bassoon or horn, both of which required a keen sense of pitch. (Later as an adult, I happily picked up the horn again.)

One of the most powerful events for me at this time was the death of my Grandmother Work in 1960, when I was 16. I will not forget the sense of loss and my uncontrollable sobbing during her funeral. I have always felt that in some way part of myself was walled up at that time to protect it from being hurt again. Many years later, this part of myself would be exposed once again.

At this time, dad was a public accountant and also had a typewriter repair business. Sometimes I helped clean typewriters. He got a motorboat, and our family would go boating on nearby Lake Texoma. After the death of his mother, he began to reevaluate his life and to plan to attend seminary in order to become a church pastor.

I also tried to wear contact lenses, but it was painful, and upon losing one, I stopped trying and have worn glasses ever since. I remember that I was anticommunist at the time. I had some good friends in school and in my neighborhood. One was named Jerry Abbott. He was very good on the trumpet. Another was Richard Wiggs. He was an excellent bassoonist. One was L. J. Gregg. He was very smart. This was the time that I wore braces to straighten my teeth. Mother and I would drive to the orthodontist in Sherman, a neighboring town in northern Texas. I was tall and skinny and had pimples on my face. I remember that I had a lot of strong emotional feelings at the time. I still was very shy. At home

I drew pictures of cars and people. I made all As and Bs in school, was in the honors society, and graduated in 1962. I had two minor car accidents due to lack of attention to my surroundings. No one was hurt.

With my family when I was in high school

My sketch of my brother Duncan

We had a second cousin Isabel Work, who was much older than our dad and taught Latin, the humanities, and the classics at Southeastern State Teachers College in Durant. She gave Duncan and me our first books on Roman and Greek mythology and also introduced us to the myth of the grandeur of the South. She was a member of the Daughters of the American Revolution and the United Daughters of the Confederacy. We loved to visit her house with its dark, musty formal living room and her little pug, Trixi. Isabel was so petite that when we saw her car driving up, it appeared that there was no driver.

I am deeply grateful to my mother and dad for providing a foundation for my life of love, ethics, and education.

4

UNIVERSITY: Profound Awakenment and Calling – Stillwater, Oklahoma

And then dad went to seminary to become a minister, and I went to university. This seemed the natural thing for me to do after high school. I went to Oklahoma State University (OSU) in Stillwater, where my father had received his master's degree in business. I thought about studying architecture or journalism, but I loved language and majored in English literature. I enjoyed the poetry of Emily Dickinson, e. e. cummings, and T. S. Elliott, among others. The first time my own poetry was published was in the university's journal, *Soliloquy*. I was influenced a great deal by my humanities professor Cyclone Covey, my political science teacher Mr. Fossick and my social psychology professor whose name I can't recall. I was impacted by Albert Camus's book *L'Etranger* (*The Stranger.*) It begins, "Mother died today or was it yesterday?" How could the character not remember such an event? I began to read another existentialist, Jean Paul Sartre. His autobiography was titled *Les Mots* (*The Words.*) I lived in Bennett Hall and later moved off campus. I attended the Wesley Foundation on campus, where the assistant campus minister, Rev. Vance Engleman, introduced me to the Ecumenical Institute (EI) and its seminar Religious Studies

1 (RS-I)—"The Theological Revolution of the Twentieth Century," which would create the trajectory of my life.

I was excited when the popular musical *West Side Story* was being rehearsed by students on campus for a performance. I loved its music, story, and dance routines. My friend John Giancola tried out for it, was selected, and joined the production. Even though I also wanted to join, I was too shy to try out. Sometimes I would sit in the theater watching the group rehearse. I sometimes wonder if my life might have developed differently if I had jumped in.

I went through what I called my existentialist period full of dark feelings, social causes like civil rights, women's rights, and peace, as well as art, music, and poetry. I helped organize campus female students to protest regulations that prohibited them from wearing pants in the library and required an early curfew in the dorms. I did not strive for the highest grades. I was having an experience. Part of my experience involved women. For the first time, women became interested in me—actually two of them— and for the first time I became interested in women—especially one. Her name was Susan Roberts. She was lovely with long, brown hair and was quite brilliant. We used to have long talks together about many things. She transferred back east to St. John's College, which was based on the Great Books Program (foundational texts of Western civilization).

The life-changing lightning bolt that struck me in 1965, when I was 21, was RS-I. I went to Chicago with a group of kids from OSU to attend the seminar. We drove up and back—a long trip. I was in the packed back seat. That was my first time to be in a large city like Chicago. The seminar took place on the West Side of Chicago in the African-American ghetto where the Ecumenical Institute had its headquarters and its demonstration community project, 5th City. The ghetto (that's what it was called then) was littered with broken glass and dilapidated cars. Many windows and doors were boarded up in the old brick buildings. Years ago, this had been an upper-class Jewish neighborhood. In 1965, it was the pits. The EI headquarters was on the old Bethany Bible School campus. There were four old buildings on campus. I slept in a bunk bed and took showers that were alternately hot and cold. I was sure that this was part of the program. The whole environment was a shock, but the seminar was an explosion within my very being.

For twenty-four hours over the weekend, we wrestled with life realities that the Christian symbols were pointing to. We were bombarded with papers by Rudolph Bultmann, Paul Tillich, Dietrich Bonhoeffer and H. Richard Niebuhr, all twentieth century theologians. We read, charted, and discussed each paper. We had conversations around questions like "What grounds you in history?"; "What would you write on your tombstone?"; "What advice would you give your friend on the way to the airport?"' "What is your image of the church?" We heard powerful, imaginal lectures about the "upagainstness" (G-O-D), about the Word of possibility—that all is good, you are accepted, the past is received, and the future is open—(the Christ word), about living a life of freedom and obedience (Holy Spirit) and about the corporateness and mission of being a social pioneer (Church). Each session began with a group conversation, then an imaginal presentation, followed by a group study and discussion of a paper. In this way, the Christian symbols and stories were demythologized so that we could encounter the life experiences and dynamics to which the symbols and stories referred.

We talked about our life experience of being driven into life and being cut off in the midst of life, of accepting the fact of our acceptance, of being 100 percent free and 100 percent obedient, and of being the sensitive, responsive part of society. We discussed a provocative painting by Picasso called *Guernica*, which depicts the Spanish Civil War. We saw and discussed a shocking movie called *Requiem for a Heavyweight*, which was about a has-been prizefighter. The conversation method for both the painting and movie involved four types of questions: What did you notice? How did it make you feel or think? What was the meaning for you? What will you decide and do differently in your life having encountered this? I was electrified. I had encountered adults who had figured it out and were telling it like it is. I experienced being accepted as the person that I was. I experienced being called to something I did not yet understand. I experienced awakening to my own mystery, depth, and greatness, and to the suffering world that was everywhere. I was also addressed by the radical intentionality of every detail of the seminar. Every coffee cup handle was turned in the same direction. Every session began on time. There was a sense of covenant and seriousness about it I had never before encountered.

When I returned to my university, I experienced myself levitating across campus (not actually, but I felt so buoyant). I was charged with a kind of electrical energy. I was bursting with new feelings, new thoughts, new questions, new challenges. Something had happened to me that I would never get over, even to this very day. I had been struck by grace. I had been awakened to the profundity of being a human being. I had experienced a vocation—a calling—and with it was to come a mission that would propel me around the world to over fifty countries.

After this experience, I completed the rest of my junior, then my senior year. I began to read more theology, philosophy, and psychology. I became fascinated with two sets of polarities. One was within Western culture—that of Apollo and Dionysus— between the rational and the sensual. The other was between Eastern and Western cultures—between rationality and dualism, and intuition and unity. I now see that these themes have never left me. I, along with many other people, have tried to make sense of these realities, both intellectually and practically within my own life.

The group of us who had taken the RS-I seminar together began to schedule events on campus to continue our own reflection and to introduce other students to this kind of awakening. This was the small beginning of my mission.

At OSU in 1966

I graduated on May 22, 1966, with a BA in English literature.

5

GRADUATE SCHOOL: Continuing the Truth Quest, and meeting Mary – Bloomington, Indiana; and Chicago, Illinois

In the summer after graduating from OSU, I returned to Chicago to attend the academy, a three-week educational program of the Ecumenical Institute. This experience created a kind of gestalt of my four years of undergraduate study into a clear, unified model of life, both theoretical and practical. After this incredible experience, I went to Bloomington, Indiana, to attend graduate school at Indiana University in the department of English. This was a beautiful campus and an excellent program, but my heart was not in it. My heart was in Chicago on the West Side. After an unsuccessful attempt to concentrate on Anglo-Saxon and linguistics, I left for Chicago to attend the Chicago Theological Seminary (CTS) on the campus of the University of Chicago (U of C) on the South Side.

My interest was not to become a minister of a local church. I wanted to study about God. I was on a quest for Truth with a capital "T." I felt that if I could not be God but only a creature, I could at least learn about Him. And I could be near the Ecumenical Institute. The U of C campus was magnificent—full of gray, Gothic buildings. Across the street from the CTS campus was Frank Lloyd Wright's famous Robbie House. Near our campus was the great Rockefeller Chapel. Drs. Thomas W. Ogletee, Andre LaCocque, and Perry LeFevre were three of my favorite professors. Also on the South Side of Chicago were some important social projects led by Saul Alinsky and Jessie Jackson. I grew a beard and smoked a pipe and wrote poetry.

With Mary Elizabeth Avery

It was here that I met Mary Elizabeth Avery. She had recently returned from the Peace Corps in Borneo in East Malaysia, where she taught English in a Chinese-speaking village. She had just transferred from a graduate program in Chinese studies with the U of C to CTS. What was it about her? Her maturity? Her sensitivity? Her brilliance? Her kind face? Her attraction to me? She was tall with brown hair, very intelligent, an Arizona State University summa cum laude history major from Phoenix, Arizona. She had written her honors thesis on the minority peoples of China. We began to have long conversations about everything under the sun, the moon, and the stars, and we began to come closer emotionally. She was my true love. When I saw her sitting one day on a bench on campus, I was struck that she was an angel. A year later, we were married and began our thirty-five-year-long conversation as we lived and worked around the world. We had been introduced by a mutual friend at CTS from South Africa, Rudolf Van Niekerk. We both attended a special seminar of the EI for seminarians, and then both decided to become university interns with the EI.

And of these first twenty-four years, how grateful I am for this beginning of my journey so filled with love by so many. I was uncertain about so many things, and yet I pressed on in trust. Where would all of this lead me and us?

PART TWO

BEING SOCIAL PIONEERS, AND LOVING POOR COMMUNITIES AS A MISSIONAL FAMILY

Conducting community, organizational, and leadership development projects with the Order Ecumenical (OE)/ Ecumenical Institute (EI)/ Institute of Cultural Affairs (ICA) while being a family: 1968 – 1990: 24 to 46 in Chicago, Malaysia, South Korea, Texas, Oklahoma, Jamaica, Venezuela

In 1968, Rev. Dr. Martin Luther King Jr. and Robert Kennedy were assassinated. Congress passed the Civil Rights Act. People took to the streets to protest the Vietnam War and to participate in the Poor Peoples' March on Washington. And NASA launched the Apollo 8 Mission.

> *"What you do makes a difference, and you have to decide what kind of difference you want to make."*
> - Jane Goodall

6

THE ECUMENICAL INSTITUTE (EI), THE ORDER ECUMENICAL (OE), AND MARRYING MARY – 5th City, Chicago, Illinois

First, Mary moved to Chicago's West Side, and I soon followed. It was January 1968. We continued to commute to CTS for classes. We saw a lot of each other. One day I asked myself what it would be like not to be with Mary? I realized that I wanted to be with her always, so I drew up a timeline showing what we would need to do and when in order to get married. I shared this with her as my proposal. She said yes. We then set to work writing our family constitution, as was the custom in the institute. I remember the line "we will manifest our love in concrete words and deeds." In August, I took her to Topeka, Kansas, to meet my parents. They loved her so much. And we went to Phoenix, Arizona, to meet hers.

On September 25 of that year, we were married in a beautiful ceremony in the Great Hall of the institute, officiated by Rev. Joseph Wesley Mathews, dean of the institute, and my father, who had become a Christian pastor after graduating from seminary following years as a teacher and public accountant. In the reception, we fed each other from a three-tiered cake. Family and friends came from Arizona, California, Kansas, and elsewhere.

Mary and my wedding reception at the Institute in 1968

Gradually, Mary's and my interests shifted entirely from CTS to the EI, and we both left seminary and became full-time interns with the EI. We, along with the EI resident community, began to study St. Teresa of Avila's *Interior Castle*, Nikos Kazantzakis's *Spiritual Exercises: The Saviors of God* and Walter Nigg's *Warriors of God*. We experimented with many kinds of liturgy and solitary offices of meditation, contemplation and prayer.

An Ecumenical Institute based in the US had been proposed by the World Council of Churches, after one was established in Bossey, Switzerland. The American EI was staffed in Chicago by faculty and students from the Faith and Life Community, which moved to Chicago from the Perkins Theological Seminary at Southern Methodist University in Austin, Texas. Joseph Mathews, the dean of the EI, had been an ethics professor at Perkins after returning from serving in World War II as a chaplain and burying many soldiers killed in battle. This experience had changed his life, and he began a journey of rediscovering the profound life meaning of the Christian symbols and story.

The staff of the EI began to talk about itself as an experimental, ecumenical, secular-religious, family order. Our vow of poverty was to live on a small stipend. The vow of obedience meant that we could be assigned anywhere in the world. And our vow of chastity was to will one thing with our lives in service to all people. Living in a secular-religious family order was challenging. Mary and I lived in a one-room apartment off campus. Each morning we woke up when it was still dark and walked to the building where we conducted our Daily Office, our liturgy. We then walked back to campus and took part in a group discussion or study (collegium). This was followed by breakfast. Then the people with outside employment left for their places of work. Mary went to the Cook County Department of Public Aid, where she was a caseworker. I stayed on campus to do my work at the EI. First, I worked in the print shop of the EI and learned how to run a printing press, collator, and cutter. The next year, after a partial thyroidectomy, I began serving as editor of the EI's publications and helped teach the two-month Global Academy—the full curriculum of the institute.

Mary and I worked with the faculty on the articulation of a New Social Vehicle and a New Religious Mode, which included the Solitaries (meditation, contemplation, and prayer), the Corporates (poverty, chastity, and obedience), and the Journeys (transparent knowing, transparent doing, and transparent being). I will never forget the deeply provocative lectures and discussions led by Joseph Mathews. Joseph was a brilliant thinker, a powerful speaker, a charismatic leader, and deeply compassionate.

We also took part in the institute's community development project in the West Side ghetto—5th City—so named for the neighborhood's Fifth Avenue. The principles on which the project was based included: 1) working with all the problems in the community; 2) working with all age groups; 3) working in a delimited geographical area; and 4) working on the depth spirit issue. The depth spirit issue we discerned on the West Side was the "victim image" of the local residents who had been disempowered over many years. We were creating a model of renewed community, in its economic, social, cultural, and political dimensions, that could be used worldwide. Later, this would be replicated in poor villages and slums in many countries around the world.

Mary and I loved going to downtown Chicago for fun. Once we saw the incomparable Rudolph Nureyev and Margot Fonteyn dance *Romeo and Juliet* with the Royal Ballet.

One New Year's eve, we were robbed at gun point on the street. Another time, someone broke into our apartment during the night but left through a window when we jumped out of bed. We became more aware that living in an impoverished community meant that we had to be detached from our own possessions.

After Dr. Martin Luther King Jr. was assassinated, an outside gang set a fire in one of the buildings on campus, but a local gang put out the fire. Mary and a few others took our colleagues' children out to the suburbs on the "El" train. After this, a few of our families decided to leave the West Side, but we and most of our colleagues decided to stay.

7

A GLOBAL ODYSSEY:
Planet Earth

In July 1969, Mary and I went on an incredible journey around the world in thirty days with a group of staff and colleagues. My Grandmother Duncan helped finance the trip for us. This Global Odyssey, as it was called, forever changed my being. It spun me around the planet and into many of the world's cultures—Mexican, Japanese, Chinese, Filipino, Thai, Nepalese, Indian, Ethiopian, Egyptian, Greek, Italian, Yugoslavian, British, Icelandic—in such a way as to indelibly mark me as a planetary citizen. I experienced the powerful mystery of the Aztecs, the sublime beauty of a Shinto shrine, the vitality of Hong Kong, the sultry weather of Manila, the serenity of the Emerald Buddha, a live-goat sacrifice in a Hindu temple (I almost fainted), a visit with a high lama in Kathmandu, the site where Buddha had his enlightenment and gave his first sermon, the devastating poverty of Calcutta, in Addis Ababa the birthday celebration of Emperor Haile Selassie, the decaying grandeur of Greek and Roman civilization, the awesome beauty of the Vatican, the wonders of a medieval walled city, a coming-home experience in the British Isles, and the eternal day of Iceland.

Planet Earth (NASA photo)

We had spent weeks preparing ourselves to be open to these cultures, and each night of the trip we wrote about and then reflected together on our experiences of the day. We were not tourists but were intent on squeezing the meaning out of our experience as we encountered humanness around the planet. I would never, ever be the same. Before this time in the first twenty-five years of my life, I had never left my native country. Suddenly in one month, I had fallen in love with planet Earth, her people, cultures, villages, cities, mountains, and seas. After this time, I was to spend seventeen years outside my own nation living in five countries and working in fifty-five.

A GIFT GIVEN

All the earth
belongs to all
the people
and living beings
that populate this
spinning ball
our planet
who else could so
claim it
except the rightful
heir
born of its soil
nurtured by its air
sustained by its waters
engaged in its toil
filled with its sights
and smells and tastes
and touched by its sorrow
awakened by its suffering
caring for its rivers and fields
longing for its life
in its fullness
God-given communion
co-creating
here and now its history

Cultures born of ecstasy
religions born of mystery
villages born of survival
cities born of complexity
nations born of tradition
languages born of joy and terror

sexes born of union
diversity and separation (glory or curse?)
the cosmic order
yet one Earth only
one humanness evolved
one past and
one future
ours
we are one
in spite of our manyness
reconciled
a gift given
received celebrated adored

Knowing that you know
what you know
- consciousness —
ecstatic union of
substance-form-and-mind
one experience
ours only (or so it seems)
our burden
to bear
for this exquisite universe
as its eyes its ears its voice
its Song of
thank you for
what was, is, and is to be
YES

After returning to Chicago from our trip, Mary and I began
to prepare to return to seminary and to move to one of the houses
of the EI in Evanston, north of Chicago. But this was not to be.
We received a phone call from Joseph Mathews while he was in

Singapore. He said, "You are needed in Kuala Lumpur, Malaysia, to replace George and Wanda Holcombe." This was the country (in East Malaysia) where Mary had lived during her Peace Corps experience. He continued, "Would you consider coming?" It took us about one second to say yes. After several weeks of preparation and waiting, off we flew into what would become eight years in Southeast and Northeast Asia overflowing with experiences and challenges and the arrival of two children to join our family. It would be twenty years before we thought again about continuing our graduate studies.

8

SOUTHEAST ASIA – EI MOVEMENT BUILDING: Petaling Jaya, Malaysia

Mary and I loved Malaysia. From our home in Petaling Jaya, we worked in Malaysia, Singapore, Thailand, and Indonesia. We discovered that we had truly received a honeymoon assignment. We also learned what it meant to build a movement. In fact, we called Don Clark, an EI colleague assigned to Singapore with his wife, Christina Welty, and asked, "Don, what is the movement?" Joseph Mathews had sent us out of Chicago to "raise up iron men (and women)." But we were not quite clear what that looked like, although we were committed to it in principle. Our colleague Vance Engleman, who had introduced me to the EI when I was in college, was assigned in Indonesia.

Malaysia was a country of Malays, Indians, Chinese, and the British; a land of tin, rubber, and Islam; of giant sea turtles, lush tropical jungles, houses on stilts, sarongs, copper-colored skin, curry, fried rice, chapati, timber lorries careening around mountain roads, former headhunters, sultans and former colonialists. My whirlwind tour of the world's cultures began to find some depth here. I was in dialogue with a richly multicultural social reality. I was infatuated. My work consisted of visiting graduates of the

International Training Institute (ITI) for World Churchmen (and women!) in Asia, which had been held in Singapore in 1969 with 102 participants from sixteen countries. The ITI's were six-week-long leadership training programs in the cultural and religious curriculum of the EI. I also began to set up RS-I seminars and Parish Leadership Colloquies (PLCs) for church leaders to provide opportunities for more people to encounter "the way life is" (twli) through the theological revolution of the twentieth century.

For Mary, however, it was another homecoming. She had previously spent two years in East Malaysia with the Peace Corps as an English language teacher in a Chinese village. While in Malaysia this time, she taught at Taylor's College, an Australian curriculum school and managed the house and family operations as well as teaching several RS-I's.

One of my memorable experiences was a trip to Indonesia to recruit for an ITI to be held in Manila. I visited with colleagues in Jakarta, as well as the fascinating city of Jogjakarta, where I experienced the mysterious gamelan orchestra and Ramayana epic in dance. I then traveled by train to Surabaya (I will never forgive myself for not visiting Bali) and on to Unjung Pandung and the northern part of Celebes, where I taught an RS-I seminar while I had a 104-degree fever. There was no one else to do it, and it had to be done. What you do when you are young and believe totally in what you are doing!

I also visited northern Thailand to recruit for the ITI. I fell in love with the charm and friendliness of the Thai people. Later I was off to Manila to help manage the operations of an ITI held in the Ateneo de Manila, a Jesuit institution.

In PJ (as Petaling Jaya was called), we lived in a beautiful house belonging to a Methodist missionary, Rev. Kjell Knutsen, who lived there with his wife, Margynell and sons Lester, Bernard, and Reinard. In the center of the house was an open garden, and the house itself was very porous to its tropical surroundings. One day we had a large snake as a visitor, and another day a Malay neighbor came over to help burn out the nest of bees that had established itself in our interior garden. This is where I began my custom of wearing a sarong as pajamas. It is also where I first experienced "jungle rot." Once, I asked a Chinese doctor if perhaps Chinese food was not sufficiently nutritious for my Western body. He laughed and said that was most certainly not the case.

Mary at the KL House

Some young Malaysians joined the team of the KL House, including Dharmalingam Vinasithamby. We also had a few Order youth who were with us for a while, including David Marshall. Some Order members assigned to India would stay with us for R & R, including Carol and George Walters. Joseph Mathews visited us once. During a reception for him, a sudden tropical rain fell, and Joseph went outside and danced in the rain while the guests watched.

In KL (as Kuala Lumpur is called), we loved to visit the National

Mosque, which looked like a space station, and the train station, which looked like a mosque. We also enjoyed eating at the many little street stalls filled with hot, steaming Chinese, Malay, and Indian taste delights. In Malaysia, you eat every few hours, at least six times a day. It is a wonderful custom. In Singapore, which we visited occasionally, there was one food area called the "car park." During the day, that is what it was, but at night it was transformed into a fabulous collection of food stalls.

I remember eating really hot Indian curry for the first time. My eyes and nose were running, and I was coughing, but I could tell it was delicious. The famous fruit "durian" was said to have one of the most unpleasant smells imaginable. I tended to agree, although many people loved its sweet taste in spite of its rotten odor.

In Malaysia I had two more car accidents. One involved another vehicle turning into my vehicle, and the other involved an oil-slickened road, a rainy day, a sharp curve in the road and a tree off the side of the road. I was not hurt, but my passenger, colleague Don Clark, from Singapore, was not so lucky. His head hit the windshield and he acquired a permanent but slight depression of one of his cheek bones. I felt responsible but also a victim of a slick road. In general, it was a beautiful experience driving on winding roads through lush jungle. Once we drove to the east coast and saw the fascinating, giant sea turtles.

We learned a few phrases in Malay. I could ask a taxi driver to take me to KL. We learned that the loud speaker at the nearby elementary school was broadcasting each morning: "ladies, gentlemen, and children, good morning."

All in all, our two years in Malaysia were very good to us—a kind of breaking into another culture at slightly more depth than our round the world in thirty days experience. I think that in Malaysia I learned that I could survive in another culture, with different foods, language, lifestyles, values, etc. I began to experience a progression that I would experience time and time again. That is the progression from hating something, to tolerating it, to rather liking it, to loving it, to craving it. This has happened to me again and again with food, music, people, and customs.

It was in Malaysia that I discovered what it meant to be of service to people of another culture, to honor them, to facilitate a life-enhancing process of self-reflection and to provide practical structures for the engagement of their new consciousness. I experienced that I was part of a global phenomenon, a global movement of the spirit, a global family. I grasped that I was very much an American, that I could not leave that behind, and that this fact had to be part of the equation of encountering-the-other. I knew that I had the interior discipline to work alone if need be and that I could trust flying off into the void—that there would be real people at the other end of the tunnel.

We also learned that we could not have children, or so a doctor told us in KL after several tests. But we kept trying. It finally produced some real results a few years and miles later in Korea. But we are not yet at that part of the story.

9

KOREA – COMMUNITY DEVELOPMENT 1, THE INSTITUTE OF CULTURAL AFFAIRS (ICA), AND CHILDREN ARRIVE!: Seoul, Kwang Yung Il Ri, and Kuh Du I Ri, Republic of Korea

After our honeymoon assignment in Malaysia, we got a phone call from Chicago telling us that we were reassigned back to Chicago. So, off we went. On the way back we stopped in Taipei, Taiwan, where we just happened to receive another phone call that kept us in Asia another six years and established our lifelong ties with the Korean people. While in Taipei, we decided to visit the EI house after a long tour of the National Museum of Chinese Art. Back at the house, the call came through from Chicago asking us to stop in Kobe, Japan, in case we were needed in Korea. So off we flew to Kobe.

We stayed several months waiting in Kobe. While we were there, we taught some English classes. This was very interesting. We had been in Kyoto and Tokyo during the Global Odyssey. It was a delight to be back in this beautiful, mysterious country of Mount

Fuji, the bullet train, sashimi, rice paper, bowing, rock gardens, huge department stores with girls in white gloves greeting you at the end of escalators, stories of samurai, tatami mats, scalding hot water baths in wooden tubs, sleeping on mats on the floor, and a real emperor. After our sojourn in Japan, we were asked to report to Seoul, and off we went. Our first night there, we almost died. But we didn't, and we lived there six wonder-filled years.

In a traditional Korean home in winter, the house is heated by yon-ton. This is a coal briquette that is lit and pushed under the floor of the house. The hot floor provides both contact heat for sitting and sleeping and some radiant heat. This system is very good but somewhat dangerous. The gas from the coal briquettes is poisonous. For this reason, it is very important not to have any cracks in your floor. The first night we were in Seoul in the EI house, the yon-ton gas leaked into our room. The next morning, we were two very sick people. We were throwing up. A doctor was called, and he hooked us up to IVs to ensure adequate hydration. It was in this position, flat on our backs, quite nauseated, that we first met our esteemed leader, Rev. Kang Byoung Hoon. He came over to welcome us to his country, to inquire about our health and to apologize for our condition. We survived and were up and fighting in the Land of Morning Calm. It was in Korea that we grew up, had our two children, became leaders, and took risks that now we look back at in amazement.

The Republic of Korea, as was common knowledge, was a truly incredible country. After some 900 invasions by foreign powers (the Japanese, Mongols, and Chinese being the most frequent), South Korea had produced in the past forty years before our arrival one of the economic miracles on our planet. And at that moment, it appeared that South Korea was also creating a political miracle with its own brand of democracy based in a Confucian sense of solidarity. Korea's strength of character comes from its 5,000-year-old culture. For centuries, Koreans have developed their own culture, learning from Chinese Confucian and Buddhist culture, and passing this culture on to the Japanese, who have in turn developed it as their own.

Korea has its own language, which is part of the Ural-Altic family of languages and is related to Turkish and Finnish. This language can be written in Chinese script or in Hangul, Korea's own alphabet, which was fashioned by the court scholars of King Sejong so that the common people could learn to read and write. Korea exalts the scholar and education within the society and has one of highest literacy rates in the world as well as institutions of excellence in higher learning.

From being the "Hermit Kingdom" to its rapid modernization and world trade position in just a few decades, South Korea's unique blend of loyalty, creativity, pragmatism, orderliness, vitality, solidarity, individualism, and sense of honor produced highly visible, dramatic results. For many nations, there was a lesson to be learned here, not so much from the particularities of Korean culture, although these were important, as from the strategy Korea has followed in basing its economic and political development on its rich culture. It was this sense of continuity with the past, combined with the necessary discontinuity of the modern era, that was Korea's hard-earned lesson.

I learned so much in Korea about so many things that it has been very difficult and challenging to do justice to this part of my story. But first of all, a bit about my life and work in this land of sages, peasants, factory workers, students, politicians, and priests, all of whom are formidable strategists.

As in Malaysia, I set about recruiting and teaching religious and cultural studies courses. I worked with Methodist and Presbyterian pastors in this endeavor—Revs. Kang Byoung Hoon, Lee Jae Joon, Kim Chong Man, Sung Chul, Chae Jong Shik, and later my dear colleague Rev. Park Si Won and many others. Mary taught in the International School of the Sacred Heart along with other of our colleagues, including Mary Ann Wainwright, Phyllis Mielke (now Hockley), Richard Sims, and Bruce and Sue Williams. Our visas were sponsored by the Korean Christian Academy, which was led by Dr. Kang Won Yong. Later, I discovered that my great-uncle, Dr. Moorman Robertson (after whom my father and I were named), had been a medical missionary with the Presbyterian Church in Korea many years earlier.

In Korea, I had many humiliating experiences. One of my most memorable took place in a PLC with a group of distinguished Presbyterian pastors wearing three-piece suits. For one of the meals, I decided to use some of my Korean language to honor the participants. So, I said, "Po ma gra." Some of the men expressed surprise. Some laughed. I thought to myself that they were pleased that I had used their language. I thought that I had said, "Let us feast." Later after that session, I asked Rev. Kim, with whom I was doing the seminar, what the participants had thought of my use of Korean. He said, "Mr. Work, do you know what you said?" I said that I thought that I had said, "Let us feast." He said, "No, Mr. Work, you said, 'Stuff it in your mouth' or 'Shovel it in.'" I was mortified. I had used language that you use with children when you are telling them to eat their rice. I had picked up this expression in our mixed Korean American household thinking that it meant "let us feast." A little learning is a dangerous thing.

Christianity is very strong in Korea. It was not introduced from the West but rather through China. The movement of church renewal that Rev. Kang Byoung Hoon was leading both with the Ecumenical Institute and through the Methodist Church was growing by leaps and bounds. We conducted many seminars all over Korea. It was a very busy, challenging time. I learned a lot about RS-I, Korea, and myself.

Many things in Korea are very strange and difficult for a Westerner. For example, sitting on the floor bends your legs in ways that are quite painful during the first several months. Also, much Korean food has an unusual taste, appearance, or smell, especially the famous kimchi, a pickled side dish of radish or cabbage served at every meal. Kimchi can be very spicy and smells strongly of fish and garlic. Actually, everything in Korea smells of garlic because everyone eats garlic every day. My journey with kimchi followed my progression of hating it, tolerating it, liking it, loving it, and finally craving it. This took several months, however.

Koreans have very strong personalities. They can be very polite, but they can also be very direct and forceful, especially when they feel that they have not been honored. I remember many occasions with Rev. Park Si Won, especially, when I was reminded that I or another of my American colleagues had not honored him. Many times, Park Si Won and I played an unacknowledged game of cultural competition. I remember one incident in the airport at Jeju City of Jeju Island. We had arrived early in the morning and were waiting to be picked up and taken to our village project site. While we were waiting, Park suggested that we have a little breakfast. I was aware that I could get a Western breakfast in the airport. Park was aware that right outside the airport terminal was a little restaurant that served typical Korean breakfast—rice, seaweed soup, kimchi and fish. I said, "Why don't we just have breakfast here in the terminal?" Park said, "Why don't we just go over to the little restaurant outside." Neither of us said that what we really wanted was a particular type of breakfast. We only argued about where we should have it. This was our game. I usually lost.

It was in 1974 that our family doubled in size. We decided to adopt a child in Korea. The Holt Adoption Agency agreed. We then discovered that Mary was pregnant (surprise, surprise). We decided to go ahead with the adoption. Stopping now would have been like an abortion to which we did not subscribe. So, we told the Holt Agency about Mary's pregnancy. Our social worker said that it was against their policy to adopt in that case. They felt that the first child should be the "natural" child and the adopted child the second. I told them that we intended to adopt a two-year-old boy before Mary gave birth. Again, our social worker said that was not possible. I asked her, "Who makes the final decision about this matter." She said "Well, I do." So, I said, "Then I am asking you to decide to let us do this." She finally agreed. We first met Kim Tae Il at the White Flower Orphanage in Taejon in July. He was sitting on the floor crying surrounded by toys. We named him Benjamin Kang, Benjamin after the Old Testament tribe and his maternal grandfather, and Kang representing his Korean ancestry and particularly after General Kang, Dr. Kang Won Yong, and Rev. Kang Byoung Hoon. Five months later on Christmas Eve, his brother, Christopher Edward, was born. He was named Christopher for the New Testament "Bearer of Christ" and Edward to represent his Anglo ancestry.

Benjamin was a cute two-year-old with straight black hair, dark brown eyes and a button nose. Christopher was a big baby with straight blond hair and green eyes. From the moment I first saw Christopher, I could sense his independent streak. It took me a few hours of processing the fact of his birth before I picked up the phone at the hospital and called my colleagues at the EI house and the Sacred Heart Convent. Since it was Christmas Eve, the Sister with whom I spoke ran through the convent shouting, "Christ is born!"

After Christopher was born, I was assigned to Japan for a few weeks to teach the Global Language School in Sendai with our colleague Kaye Hayes (Kaze Gadway). Suddenly, sharing my life and our one room with these two little creatures had become a psychic strain on me. When I returned home I was better able to take up my new role as a dad with gusto. How could I have let Mary deal with all of that without me? Fortunately, there were many colleagues in the house who also helped out.

In the summer of 1975, the four of us returned to the US for one month. Mary had to have an operation for cancer of her eyelid; we also visited our families, and Benjamin became a naturalized American citizen.

Our family traveling from Seoul to Chicago

In addition, we attended a Global Research Assembly in Chicago in which the Institute decided to launch the three campaigns of Global Community Forum (awakenment), Global Social Demonstration (engagement), and the Intra-global Movement (fulfillment). This was our "turn to the world" to show the historical church what it looked like to care for society. Increasingly, we worked under the name of the Institute of Cultural Affairs (ICA), a new legal entity we created, rather than the Ecumenical Institute, in order to have a secular rather than a religious face. Several years later, ICA received consultative status with the United Nations Economic and Social Council.

After a few years of teaching religious and cultural weekend courses, including RS-I's and PLC's, and six-week-long International Training Institutes (ITI's) in Seoul and Hong Kong, the institute and we in particular began talking about the necessity of "demonstrating the love of God" to society. This was after many years of attempting to awaken the church to its profound task of caring for the world by recruiting people to attend our religious and cultural courses. We had never been missionaries trying to convert people to Christianity. Finally, the institute decided that we ourselves must show the way. We must go out into the world and demonstrate "human development" among the poorest of the poor. For this, we decided to initiate projects at the village level in each of the twenty-four time zones of the world. In Korea, we decided to begin a project on Jeju Island, the poorest, most remote province in South Korea.

Many of the villages of Jeju were still in the twelfth century, complete with pig toilets, thatched roofs, mud floors, rock walls, and the local version of animism. We first conducted an ITI in Jeju City and then a consultation to create the project plan. At the time, we thought that we were creating a project for the entire Island. But after the consult, Joseph Mathews visited, and we heard the words, "You must find a village." This was quite a shock. None of us had any experience in or with villages at that time. We had read Schumacher's book *Small Is Beautiful*. We knew that the most abject poverty was found in rural villages. But we had not thought to locate the project in a village. We found a village, Kwang Yung Il Ri, on the slopes of Mount Halla, overlooking fields of yellow flowers, which swept down to the sea, where white waves crashed on the black volcanic rock. Joseph's advice to us was, "When you live in the village, you will experience a spiritual crisis." He was ever so right.

I will never forget the day I moved our few belongings to Kwang Yung Il Ri, into our rough rock walls and thatch-roofed house. It was raining lightly. The road from Jeju City to the village was rocky and bumpy. Later when Mary, Benjamin and Christopher arrived, I think that I was already in shock. I had never lived without the sights, lights, sounds, comforts, and conveniences of modern urban life, whether in a small town in Oklahoma or a great city like Seoul or Chicago. I felt as if I had died. The sensory deprivation was so great, the disorientation so complete. Living in a bizarre landscape, seascape, and cloud scape, in a bizarre culture, we were faced with an impossible task of assisting the villagers in transforming their village within two years. The Kim Chong Man family was equally in shock. Even though they were Korean, they were Seoulites. We set about working in various guilds. I was in the agricultural guild. I knew nothing about agriculture. I was not fluent in the Korean language. But there I was catalyzing socio-economic change with my very being and that of my little family.

The high point of each week was riding the bus over the bumpy road to Jeju City to have our one hot bath of the week. Once, Christopher developed mouth sores and could not eat or drink. We rushed him into the city and returned to the village greatly relieved that he was much better. Both boys fell on the rocky land in the village so often that their little legs were permanently covered in cuts, bruises, and scars. Once, Benjamin fell and chipped his front tooth. In winter it was bitterly cold. We were never entirely warm. Later we lived in a little house with two other families, each family of three or four members in one room with sliding paper walls between us. We learned to respect each other's privacy—which became a matter of decision rather than a physical reality I participated in many rituals of birth and death involving much food, fruit, and drink, not only for those of us present but for the spirits as well. When we were building our training center in the village, the villagers conducted a ritual using chicken blood to cleanse and protect the space.

As I remember these days, I find that I am shocked that I did this. What sustained me in the midst of so much discomfort and disorientation was that I was living out of the most powerful story I could imagine. I was part of a global servant force that was creating signs of human development in the twenty-four time zones of our planet. Surely, this was worth all of the difficulties and doubts. But what is even more shocking is that I did this as a family with two small children and a wife. I did not do it as a solitary monk but as a missional family. My family will always be this family that lived in Kwang Yung Il Ri.

Christopher, on the right, in the village

The year after the project began, we were reassigned to Seoul. We were then the directors of the Institute of Cultural Affairs (ICA) in Korea. Rev. Kang was Area Tokyo director for Japan and Korea. Although everyone thought it was impossible, a fundraising I launched was able to raise several tens of thousands of dollars for the project from Korean companies. I was also a member of the Seoul Rotary Club, where I met heads of major Korean companies such as Gold Star. It was then that Joseph, Kang, and our team decided to host a World's Fair of Human Development in Kwang Yung Il Ri. This task seemed overwhelming at the time. But Kang, Park, and I, and many others worked to make it a reality. Joseph had worked unflaggingly to make the "Band of 24" a reality. This event was the symbol of that victory.

It was after this celebration and the following Global Research Assembly that Joseph was diagnosed as having terminal cancer of the pancreas.

We received a phone call from Chicago that Joseph Mathews

had died. Following Korean custom, we immediately set up an altar with his picture draped in black and with incense and candles. House members and colleagues came to pay their respects at this shrine. Then Kang, Park, Mary, and I flew to Chicago with our sadness and grief to attend his funeral. What an awesome event this was. His body was cremated, and his ashes were put in an unmarked box, no name and no date, with the Order cross on it. Into this box were placed his silver ring and blue shirt, symbols of the Order, and his cross, a symbol of the historic church. We celebrated his life and death in the context of the Daily Office, the institute's great, ecumenical liturgy. For me (and for many others), Joseph was the most powerful, spirit-filled person I had ever known. I will always be grateful for his life, his message, his passion, his vision, his compassion, his very being. I suppose that I feel a special responsibility for having known him, a responsibility to continue in some fashion his work, his vision, his mission. I believe that now it has somehow become my very own vision and mission.

Rev. Kang, 1ˢᵗ row center; Rev. Park, 1ˢᵗ row right; with other colleagues

The last year I was in Korea, we launched a second Human Development Project near the demilitarized zone north of Seoul in the village of Kuh Du I Ri. Now, Park Si Won was director. He did a magnificent job of leading the project team. This village became an outstanding example of local development with its credit union, community center, piggery, green houses, museum, preschool, and health center. This was an embodiment of the theological revolution of addressing suffering through new social structures as those who care.

My family lived in one room behind the village store in the newly constructed community center. Park's family of four lived in one room on the other side of the center. Every morning, Mary and Benjamin rode a bicycle from the village to the town and caught a bus to Seoul, where Mary was a teacher at Sacred Heart International School and Benjamin was a student. Christopher and I stayed in the village. Once, Christopher got lost. Rev. Park made an announcement over the village loudspeaker, and we located him. One morning a filmmaker was in the village to make a documentary on the project for IT&T, which had provided a large grant. Benjamin was playing in the rice paddy and suddenly began to cry and shout. He had stepped on a large piece of glass, which had gone up into his leg. Mary walked into town with Benjamin on her back while the cameras rolled (we had no vehicle).

I learned how to plant rice in the paddy fields. In water up to our ankles, we walked along the rough muddy field bending again and again to insert shoots of rice plants down in the mud. This was also the time when Mary and I began to talk about needing to return to the US. We had been in Korea about six years. We felt a great love for Korea but an even greater loyalty to our Order. We felt that if we stayed any longer in Korea, we would never leave. We left for Chicago in July 1978. I remember how much I cried when we left. I was still bowing to people two years later. So much growth, so much learning, so much pain, so many thoughts, and feelings, I will always be part Korean.

10

USA – ICA COMMUNITY DEVELOPMENT 2: Dallas, Texas; Indiahoma, Oklahoma

We flew back to Chicago, visiting our parents in Arizona and Oklahoma on the way. We received an assignment to Salt Lake City. We left for San Francisco, then on to Salt Lake City and then to Denver. It was decided that there would not be an EI house in Salt Lake City, so we were then reassigned to Dallas, and off we went. During all of this moving about, I was still longing for my lost Korea. Who was I? Where was I headed?

Dallas was a big city with lots of freeways. I had not driven a car for six years, or rather, I had driven a jeep on country roads. I religiously avoided the superhighways in Dallas, using every possible back way to get around the city. It was overwhelming. Everything was so fast and glittering in "Big D." Our colleagues were very patient with us as we readjusted to the US, still feeling like Koreans. We quickly found a Korean restaurant in Dallas. We lived in a big two-story house that was owned by the group of colleagues in the Dallas region, including Dane and Glenda Adkinson. My family had a several-room apartment upstairs and our own bathroom. I was in culture shock. For the past ten years my family had lived in one room—first the two of us and then the four of us. I felt almost nauseous with all of the space. My work consisted of circuiting north Texas and Oklahoma setting up and facilitating town meetings in small communities. Mary had a job with the American Arbitration Association.

Each town meeting began by asking community members what challenges did their community face. They would brainstorm and group these into a few major challenges such as distant health care facilities. The community would then brainstorm actions that would deal with these challenges, such as creating a local clinic. Community members would also create a story, song, and symbol for their community to provide motivation for working together to improve their community. The ICA held a town meeting in every county in the US to mark the 200th anniversary of the nation.

The next year, we were assigned to direct an ICA Human Development Project in Indiahoma, Oklahoma. Finally, I was back in my home state. Indiahoma was a little town that had been dying for some time in southwestern Oklahoma near the Wichita Mountains and Lawton. The institute had begun a project there the year before. About half of the people of Indiahoma were members of the Comanche tribe, and the other half were white. It was a poor little town.

We jumped in and began working with the mayor, Barbara Bailey, and with the school and the health center. We received a Volunteers in Service to America (VISTA) project, which I directed. We helped fix up an old building as a community center. We wrote a two-year report on all of the changes in the community. The town built a new water tower, a new welcome sign, and began many new activities. I often could not stop myself from bowing to people as Korea was still in my bones.

New welcome sign

The highlight for us was setting up and holding the Festival of Hometowns, complete with marching band, horses, floats, and booths. I was very touched by the Comanche customs, dances, and style of being in Indiahoma. Growing up in Oklahoma, I had never really become familiar with the Native American traditions. Now I was living them. I danced in a Comanche ceremony. Benjamin and Christopher had many native friends. We visited the museum that tells of the life of the famous Apache, Geronimo. Many times, we drove through the nearby wildlife reserve and saw buffalo and groundhogs. A year later we got a phone call.

11

CARIBBEAN – ICA COMMUNITY DEVELOPMENT 3, AND GRANDMOTHER'S PASSING: Woburn Lawn, and Kingston, Jamaica

We were needed urgently in Jamaica to replace Larry and Mary Ward. Could we go within three weeks? The answer was yes. We took the boys out of school—it was February—packed and moved to Jamaica. We had known nothing of or about Jamaica. Before we got there, we began reading a few books about it. It seemed fascinating—dreadlocks, beautiful beaches and mountains, extreme poverty, a former British colony, former slaves, English speaking. Once again, I experienced that familiar anxiety of leaving the known and flying off into the unknown with new demands to be encountered.

We were the directors of the ICA for the Caribbean area and the recently launched Woburn Lawn Human Development Project. The night we arrived, we rode in the back of an old van up a winding road in the Blue Mountains, east of Kingston, to a little village named Woburn Lawn. We moved our few belongings into two tiny rooms of a little frame house in the village. Immediately we were at work.

The village project had been set in motion before we arrived by a weeklong community consultation, resulting in many community taskforces such as a builders guild, youth group, and women's group, and initiatives such as a preschool, health clinic, and a cooperative.

Working with a high-powered steering committee, I began setting up a national conference on human development in the 1980s called the Jamaican Potential. Mary began to familiarize herself with the operations in Woburn Lawn, particularly the multipurpose cooperative and management of grants from the European Community and the Inter-American Development Bank.

We put our two sons in the village school. It had one room with 300 children in eight classes separated by blackboards. All of the children were, of course, black with the exception of our two— one Korean and one white. Our house was at top of the village, and the boys school was at the bottom of the village. The village was almost vertical, along the mountainside. Up and down we would walk with aching leg muscles.

The countryside was gorgeous—lush green forests, plentiful fruit trees, including mango and avocado, brightly colored flowers, including hibiscus, fresh mountain air, tiny hummingbirds, called "doctor birds," river prawns, the blazing tropical sun. It was kind of a natural paradise. It was here that the descendants of slaves who had worked the coffee plantations now lived in their little villages.

Jamaican Blue Mountain coffee was one of the most expensive in the world. One reason for this was its flavor—sweet and nutty— and another was that there was such a limited quantity. The Japanese bought most of it. It was easier to get a cup in Tokyo than in Kingston. But the villagers were not getting rich growing coffee. Their plots were too small. And the government bought all of the coffee and exported it.

The leader of Woburn Lawn was Alice Wright, the school principal. What a great lady! We learned so much working with her. She was a true friend and colleague. She was a tireless worker for her community, her school, where she was principal, and for her family of two children. The other great lady with whom we worked was the president of ICA Jamaica Ltd., Icelyn Seaton, former permanent secretary of the Ministry of Youth and Community Development. What a wise woman! I enjoyed working with her so much. In Korea, I had learned to work with strong men. In Jamaica, I learned to work with strong women, including Sybil Francis and Pansy Hart in Kingston, and Anabel Crosdale in Woburn Lawn.

Anabel Crosdale, and volunteers

There were also strong men in Jamaica, of course, such as Busti, head of the village builders guild, and BJ. The Honorable Errol Anderson, minister of youth and community development, was also our colleague in the development task. And there were many others.

When we arrived, we were told that Jamaica was a hardship

assignment. Somehow, we embraced the situation and stayed four fantastic years. In fact, we discovered that "hardship" can be a self-fulfilling prophecy and that other stories can be told about any situation. We found Jamaica to be an exhilarating place to live and work. Of course, there were many difficulties, especially physical ones in the village. But there was also the beauty of the place and the boundless vitality of the people. There was chaos, but there was also an underlying orderliness about human relationships arising out of a culture of slavery and British propriety.

Our two sons quickly learned patois, the special dialect of Jamaica, a blend of English, West African, Spanish and slavery language. They also learned to dance reggae like village boys. They really became Jamaicanized.

Benjamin with his friend Freddie in the village

I fell in love with many things Jamaican. This was after my usual progression of hating it, tolerating it, liking it, loving it and finally craving it. This included ackee, a local fruit, and salt fish, black goat stew, Red Stripe beer, the winding mountain roads, the blaring speakers of reggae music, dancing reggae, the sudden rainstorms and the blazing sun. The first year I was there I must admit that I found the seeming lack of formality to the begetting of children very offensive. Pregnant women were simply called "baby mothers." Often, the fathers were unknown or in dispute. The women raised the children. The fathers, if they stepped forward, would offer some occasional monetary support. At first, this seemed a beastly way of forming a society. Later, I grew to see the underlying form, the genuine love and care of children, and the basis of the customs flowing out of the days of slavery, when only the white folks could get married. Jamaica had developed its own ways of being human that in many ways are more "human" than more formal but alienated structures of the family. But Jamaica was also in evolution. Where all of this would go depended upon many internal and external factors.

My parents visited us. It was wonderful showing them around and being with them in Jamaica.

After the Jamaican Potential, we created a new legal entity called ICA Jamaica, Ltd., and launched the Blue Mountain Cluster—a project involving sixteen nearby villages. We conducted a Human Development Training Institute to train local leaders. We got grants from the Canadian International Development Agency and the Rotary Foundation. The work expanded to other clusters of villages in the Blue Mountains. The young Jamaican staff, including Winston Davis, Donrad Duncan, Leon Crosdale, and volunteers Percy, Horace, and others, worked hard on their circuits, setting up and conducting community forums and assisting the villagers with small economic and social projects. We also had international staff, including Agak Nyapodi, and overseas volunteers, including Rotarians, and Joy Jinks and her daughter.

We established an ICA house in Kingston, the capital, and put our sons in the international school. They also enjoyed studying taekwondo. Mary, although now based in Kingston, was still in charge of the village projects in the Blue Mountains, grant monitoring, staff relations, and the ICA office in Kingston.

One of my most satisfying experiences was working on Jamaica's participation in the International Exposition of Rural Development (IERD), an initiative of ICA headquarters, and all national ICAs. This was a three-year process, involving fifty countries around the world, of putting the spotlight on success. The IERD was sponsored by, in addition to ICA, several other international organizations, including the United Nations Development Program (UNDP) and UNICEF. In Jamaica, we held a Rural Development Symposium, documented many projects, raised funds and sent a delegation of fifteen Jamaicans to the global plenary in New Delhi, India, including the minister of youth and community development, The Honorable Ed Bartlett. We also had one delegate from Haiti, following a visit I made to Port au Prince, in which I discovered the resilience and hard work of the Haitian people in the face of extreme poverty. Working with Jamaica's IERD National Steering Committee was a great challenge and honor for me.

I also marketed and helped facilitate strategic planning seminars with organizations including the National Commercial Bank, the interministerial Basic Services for Children's Project sponsored by UNICEF, the Diocese of Jamaica and the Girl Guides. Teaching a course on community development at the University of the West Indies was another enjoyable experience.

All in all, I felt that I was making a contribution to the history of development in the nation of Jamaica. But once again, the great Assignments Wheel turned, and up came the nation of Venezuela. It was also in our last year in Jamaica that I began reading about the "new paradigm." Among the many books I read were *The Tao of Physics* and *The Dancing Wu Li Masters*— two books about the new physics and the philosophical implications. There was something utterly fascinating and disturbing about what I was reading and thinking. I remember asking myself, "But what difference does all of this make in one's daily existence?"

Before this happened, however, Mary and I were back in Chicago for the Council of a Lifetime. Our group had been planning this for many years, and virtually all of our members were present. This was quite an event for us all. It was in this council that we turned our attention to the "new paradigm" and to the practice of "insight meditation." This new openness, both intellectual and spiritual, began to have profound consequences on who we were becoming, both as a group and as individuals. It was in this council that we decided to "build the Order" and to work in four networks—development, economic, education and planetary unity. This was the beginning of much tension and confusion about the mission or missions of our group. At the time of this council, I was furious at those in our midst who were forcing these changes and even denying our sense of continuity with our past. As I look back now, I believe that these changes were indeed necessary both for our group as a whole and for each one of us as individuals.

My Grandmother Duncan passed away on January 16, 1984, in Durant, Oklahoma. Because we were overseas, we could not attend her memorial service. I loved her very much.

12

VENEZUELA – ICA COMMUNITY DEVELOPMENT 4, AND WHOLE SYSTEM TRANSITION: Caracas, and Caño Negro, Venezuela

I arrived in Caracas on the night of September 1, 1984, with my ten-year-old son, Christopher, in tow. Mary was wrapping things up in Jamaica, and Benjamin was staying on in Chicago at the institute's residential learning center.

We took a taxi to the poor barrio of Las Minas de Baruta, where the institute had partial use of a community center. When we arrived at 1 a.m., I tried to rouse people in the building but to no avail. We spent our first night in Venezuela in the nearby Holiday Inn.

The institute had a human development project in the cacao-growing region of Barlovento with its black population, an hour and a half east of Caracas. All of our staff were there except for one or two who were in Caracas to raise donations. The Cano Negro Human Development Project was part of the band of 24 projects around the world in the 24 time zones and was the first project in Latin America. Mary and I were assigned as the directors of the institute's work in Venezuela, northern South America and the nation of Brazil. Later, Jamaica and the rest of the Caribbean were put under our care. Caracas was also designated as the senior office for Latin America and one of the global centers of the institute. This was a big responsibility.

We soon discovered that our staff were suffering from low morale due to the unscheduled departure of the previous director. We quickly began to bolster our sense of what the institute was in this society. Also because of the role of Fathers Rafael Davila, Bob Rank, and Marcel Rainville, three Catholic priests working with the institute, there was a strong identification with the Catholic Church. We decided that the institute's future was to be secular.

I knew no Spanish, and here began five and one-half years of struggle to learn another language, after years of making no similar attempt. In fact, when we were in Korea, our corporate culture discouraged learning the local language for fear of becoming part of the local scene rather than maintaining ones "pedagogical distance." In addition to our Venezuelan staff, Tina Valdez (now Spencer), one of the senior staff from the US, was fluent in Spanish.

How could I tell this part of the story, which was still so vivid and fresh in my life, so filled with pain and transformation?

We soon discovered that the institute had little money, no active board of directors, no programs set up, low morale, and no urban base. We set about changing all of that.

One program we were able to concretize in the first two months was under the sponsorship of a government oil company, Maraven. The program involved conducting six weeks of work in the village of San Diego de Cabrutica, in the oil fields of Zona Zuata near the Orinoco River. Off I went, knowing no Spanish, with two of my Venezuelan colleagues, Jacobo Pacheco and Antonio Beltran. We lived in a little llanero (prairie) town, set up a steering committee, conducted a series of leadership training sessions and a foro comunitario (community forum) for the whole town and followed up by helping start small projects all the while liaising with the local Maraven officials.

Ramona and Jacobo Pacheco, ICA Venezuela staff

At night, by a dim light and with my mosquito coils burning, I read *Cosmos* by Carl Sagan and *The Lives of a Cell* by Lewis Thomas. I learned to delight in the music of the llanero harp played by our neighbor across the street. I enjoyed the local cooking, the hot sun, the joropo dance, the iguana that visited our living room; even the cold showers were somehow refreshing. This was my plunge into one of the local cultures in the interior. But another part of the dialogue continued with the "new paradigm," and my question remained, "What does this have to do with my daily life?" I somehow felt very deeply that it did but I could not as yet see it or articulate it.

When I returned to Caracas I was still excited with my recent adventure, but now the huge task of building a viable organization faced me. I often wished that I were back in Jamaica, where I could speak English and where I had been "successful." Why had I been called to the continent of South America? Who were these

Spanish-speaking people? What was my relationship to them as a North American?

In 1985, we moved most of our staff from the village of Caño Negro to the city of Caracas and lived in two rented apartments in the barrio of Las Minas. We had to borrow the money to rent the apartments from the president of ICA, Father Marcel Rainville, a Catholic priest. We continued our work in Barlovento and with Maraven in Zona Zuata, working in four other small towns over the next two years. We began to create an active group of advisers, which was to evolve into our active board of directors.

I also began to conceptualize a large, three-year project in partnership with the Rotary Foundation. I wrote a grant proposal and submitted it to the foundation through one of our colleagues, Jamil Dunia, who was a Rotarian of international stature. The next year, the foundation approved a grant of over $400,000 for the project. The ICA and the Antimano Rotary Club began to attempt to solidify a partnership in order to activate the project. It was not, however, destined to be; a year later, after much misunderstanding and several false starts, the grant offer was withdrawn by the foundation at the request of the local club. This two-year effort was filled with pain and frustration and made me less interested to pursue such development partnerships in the future.

We built a strong board of directors for ICA Venezuela, including banker Alejandro Lara as president, John Lawton as vice president, Teresa Sosa, and others. We established an office in downtown Caracas in Altamira. And we also had some high-level advisers, including Jose Antonio Gil, Ivan Lansberg, and Gustavo Roosen.

But something else was rising in my life, and it had to do with consciousness and the search for the Beloved. In the summer of 1986, Mary and I attended the Planetary Vision Quest sponsored by the ICA in Chicago. In particular, one seminar on Sacred Psychology led by Dr. Jean Houston, awoke a dying vision, rekindled an extinguished flame, retouched parts of my body, mind and spirit that had become encrusted in layers of self-protection and insensitivity. It was then that I sensed I was being called yet again to another place, another rhythm, yet very much connected to my "pollen path" of the past twenty-one years. I began to stretch, to dance, to fall into deep meditation, to read more of the literature of the "new paradigm." Some deep essence was awakening; some deep resonance was being established that would not leave me alone. Try as I had, I could not shake off this new sense of being, this new, radical aliveness that called for all of my knowing, my doing, and my being.

Following this event, we traveled to Bilbao, Spain, for the institute's Global Council. Here, in the land of St. Ignatius of Loyola, St. Teresa of Avila, and St. John of the Cross, our little band met once again to map out our future. We were going to set up adequate facilities, adequate financing for our lives and work, market our products, clarify our reason for being and catalyze social research concerning the two questions of "What is humanness?" and "What is development?" These two questions, posed for our group by Dr. Joseph van Arendonk of UNFPA, captured my imagination. While we were in Bilbao, our dear colleague Paul Bosch died of a heart attack in Caracas while working to save the Rotary project.

When we returned to Caracas, we launched our new plans without much success. In the midst of one more cash flow crisis and with the Rotary project clearly heading for the rocks, we invited Jean Houston to Caracas to conduct two seminars. We had no idea how Venezuelans would react to her message or style. We had no idea if we could make the kind of profit we needed from these events. But we continued marketing and preparing. Colleague Linda Jones (now Sunny Walker) was instrumental in all of this. Finally, in March of 1987, we experienced the exhilaration and challenge of success—financial, yes, but, moreover, spiritual, personal, and social.

Over 120 people attended Jean's two seminars on "The Possible Human" and "Sacred Psychology." The ICA did a traveling seminar with Jean to Barlovento that was filled with mystery, healing, and many connections. We also met with leaders in education such as Dr. Luis Alberto Machado, former minister of intelligence, and Dr. Beatriz de Capdeveille, concerning the future of education in Venezuela.

Personally, I experienced Jean as one of the most brilliant, creative people I had ever known. The processes and exercises she orchestrated in her workshops released new levels of energy and insight into my own life and the lives of many others. These processes activated four levels of a person's experiences—the sensory/physical, psychological/historic, mythic/symbolic, and unitive/spiritual. I felt confirmed and challenged by her statement that our lifestyle had created in some of us great "flexibility of psyche."

This was also the month that we purchased and moved into Quinta Los Bosquecillos, a 23-room mansion in Caracas, that was to be the home of our Order. At that time, I did not imagine that in two years our Order would be called out of being by our leadership, including myself.

Our family in Caracas

Also in 1987, we did our first program for a private company in Venezuela—a six-session series of strategic planning for Colgate Palmolive. Coming out of so many years of community development work and being part of a secular-religious order, I put together and trained a team of consultants that included three villagers who did not have high school diplomas, and two young Americans, neither of whom had a university degree. The first two seminars were operationally successful, but the human resource director was furious at the makeup of our team. "When I looked around the room, I couldn't believe it. Two of your people were black! And one of them had a terrible, uncultured accent!" I learned painfully that the "world" had different standards than I did. For the remaining four seminars, I reluctantly altered the makeup of our team.

We also did seminars for the Venezuelan American Chamber of Commerce, the Venezuelan American Friendship Association, FCB, Citibank (in Trinidad, Miami and Colombia) and the Senior Foundation. Our teams of facilitators were acceptable and did an excellent job.

At the end of 1987, we hosted a lecture series on social development by Dr. Willis Harman, the president of the Institute of Noetic Sciences in the US, and a seminar on education by Dr. Robin Van Doren. We also decided to participate in a Whole Systems Transformation (WST) experiment with the Long Term Investment Team of the institute from Chicago.

In January 1988, I traveled to Mexico City to help plan a global ICA conference "Our Common Future." This is the first time I heard from one of my colleagues the expression, "the Order is dead." I was shocked. How could this be—the group I had been part of for twenty years? But something in me silently acknowledged the existential truth of this simple statement. Why and how I did not know, but that and what I sensed. Later that year, the global Panchayat, our guiding body residing in Hong Kong, proposed that all global Order structures be taken out of being. Over the years, we had evolved from a Christian-ecumenical spirituality to a secular understanding. We were not financially self-sufficient and had no pension funds. And our mission had changed from renewing the church to demonstrating renewed community to social transformation within a new paradigm. We could no longer support a global core group of families to staff ICAs around the world. Rather, we had to empower each local unit to be self-supporting and self-directing. National ICAs could continue but without an Order core.

Also in January, our house in Caracas had a conversation about "What if we had all the money we needed for our life and mission; what difference would it make to you?" It was then that we, and I, decided that we were going to go for the money that we needed—that was prerequisite for doing what we had decided to do. Always before, money had been a mere instrumentality—that which we attracted by our vision and our plans and projects. Vision and action first, then the money will follow.

In April, we held a consultation to launch our WST experiment. The team that came from Chicago to work with us included Bill and Lyn Mathews Edwards (the late Joseph Mathews's former wife) and Raymond Spencer. We asked the "wise old man or woman within" to reveal to us the pathways of transformation. And he/she did. There were three pathways, and we were off and running. We established two professional divisions, one for community development and one for organizational development. We also began to restructure our finances to empower "individuation." By August, we were all on competitive salaries for the first time in our institute experience.

Mary and I moved our family out of the ICA house to an apartment in downtown Caracas. This was to symbolize that indeed the order was dead and we were all in a new mode of being.

One of our amazing stories of 1988 had to do with a research project titled "Corporate Culture, Venezuelan Culture and Effective Management." This project grew out of a challenge given me by one of our advisers, Ivan Lansberg, the chairman of a group of corporations. We then collaborated with Dr. Susan de Vogeler to develop and execute the project. What an education for us all! We learned so much about organizations in Venezuela. I learned a great deal from Susan, who had her PhD in organizational theory from MIT.

We also got a large contract with Household Mortgage Services (HMS) in Chicago through a colleague in ICA Jamaica. Since the WST consult, he had been part of our division of organizational development called ICA Associates. This contract made our organizational transformation possible. It totaled for that year around $100,000 in gross revenue. I flew to Chicago twice and to Tampa twice to do programs with HMS. I felt like an international consultant. But we were on thin ice, and in November we fell through. Our ICA Jamaica colleague withdrew from ICA Associates, taking HMS with him, and moved to Washington, D.C.

It seemed like the end of the world. And I was angry. My new career as an international consultant with the private sector seemed to be short lived.

Everything had to change. There was no longer enough money to cover our budget. We had to lay off staff. Just a few months earlier, these people had been loyal Order members. Suddenly, they were redundant personnel. We were taking a head-count reduction. Our corporate culture had radically changed overnight. Starting in January 1989 and in great pain, we began to follow this strategy. We were acting like a business, and I was acting as the tough CEO. There was a particularly painful situation with one family. When the husband had to be laid off, his wife followed him. One year later, we were barely on speaking terms. We had been fellow members of an Order for fifteen years. What had happened to our culture? What had happened to me? Why was I acting like a manager when the day before yesterday I was a prior of a family Order?

The year 1989 was one of the most difficult in my life—a

year of trying to make a new structure work. More people were laid off. Other people resigned. There were a few bright spots in the year. One of them was the continuation of the corporate culture research project. Another was a great seminar in Caracas for forty executives, which we marketed for Harrison Owens, an expert in organizational transformation from the US. But then Susan de Vogeler left the corporate culture project to start her own company. Our office manager and bookkeeper resigned. We no longer had sufficient income to maintain our level of salaries and operations. Something more had to happen.

In November, I announced to our staff that the new ICA structures were not working. Our three remaining salaried staff would need to resign and go on honoraria like our two other staff. When I reported this to the president of ICA Venezuela, Alejandro Lara, a Caracas banker, his reaction was, "Well, if ICA can't make it, we will liquidate and stop." I guess I had expected and hoped for more commitment and fight.

In December, Jose Elias Graffe and I attended Jean Houston's Mystery School in New York and a Whole Systems Transformation (WST) Think Tank with Jean. I had prepared a paper on the "Whole Systems Transformation of Venezuela" based on the findings of our corporate culture research project. The think tank members began the writing of a book about WST. I also visited my family in the US, my oldest son, my parents, parents-in-law, and my brother's family. This was a time of listening intently for advice. I was in great need of advice. What was I to do with the rest of my life? Where was I headed?

When I returned to Caracas, Mary and I spent the twelve days of Christmas talking about our future. We decided to go to San Diego, California; then we decided to go to New York City; then we decided that we would stay in Venezuela and make money in order to move toward our vision of our own home in the US, graduate school, adequate family income, schooling for our two sons, studying with Jean Houston, and writing.

At the beginning of 1990, we were in yet another period of transition. We sold ICA Venezuela's major asset, Quinta Los Bosquecillos, the 23-room mansion that used to be the Order's home. All of the funds were deposited and remained in ICA Venezuela's bank account. We exposed our board members to the actual situation, so that they and others could think and decide about the future of ICA in Venezuela. Mary had a job offer from the Colegio Intemacional de Caracas. It would have allowed her to teach, which she loved, to study for her master's, to cover Christopher's school fees and to earn a small salary. However, after much reflection, discussion, and planning, we both decided it was time to return to the US with the highly capable Venezuelans in charge of ICA Venezuela.

And what of me? I no longer felt like a big consultant or the prior of an order. Who was I? What was I going to do next? Which void charged with energy was I going to jump into, as I had done time and time again in my life? What about my little family? What was our destiny? Or was it to be each one's destiny? It seemed that the die had been cast on individuation. Was there no turning back? No return to a simpler, more corporate, unconscious mode?

On 16 March, I wrote in my journal: "What I am going through is a common human experience—a depression related to a life crisis of a change of country, job, self-image and status, doubts and questions about identity—who am I? vocation—what do I? and lifestyle—how be I? and anxiety about the future."

This reluctant revolutionary was deciding once against to jump into the creative void.

PART THREE

SERVING SLUMS, CITIES, AND COUNTRIES, AND CELEBRATING LIFE AND DEATH

Providing global, national, and city policy advice in decentralized governance with the United Nations Development Program (UNDP): 1990 – 2006: 46 to 62 in New York; and Planet Earth

In 1990, the Berlin Wall was torn down. Nelson Mandela was released from prison after 27 years and became president of South Africa. The Hubble Space telescope was launched into orbit providing awe-inspiring views of the universe.

> *"From time to time, one sees the possibility of the world as it could be, where each of us has the opportunity to live life fully and to have our lives make the kind of difference we want to make. Focusing our attention, daily and hourly, not on what is wrong but on what we love and value, allows us to participate in the birth of a better future, ushered in by the choices we make each and every day."*
> -Nelson Mandela

13
NYU MEGA-CITIES PROJECT: New York City

On March 28, 1990, Mary, Christopher, and I left Venezuela, and returned to the United States. Benjamin was in high school in San Francisco, living with his aunt Marjorie and uncle John. We thought that we were headed toward San Diego, but New York City captured us. At my request, Jean Houston introduced me to her editor and literary agent in New York. Also, George Walters, an ICA colleague in New York, talked with us about possibilities in New York and then offered me a part-time job with the Mega-Cities Project at New York University—a project linking 14 of the world's largest cities.

New York City

Christopher finished the eighth grade in a New York public school. Benjamin graduated from George Washington High School in San Francisco and was accepted to the University of California at Santa Barbara (UCSB) on full scholarship. Mary visited her parents, whom she had not seen in four years. She then returned to New York to orchestrate the renovation of our apartment in a building on the Lower East Side of Manhattan, where the ICA had been based for years. I continued participating in the Whole System Transformation (WST) Think Tank, and Mary and I took turns attending various sessions of the Mystery School. We joined an Episcopal church, St. Mark's Church-in-the-Bowery, a community alive with spiritual growth, social concern, intellectual questioning, and artistic expression in poetry, dance, and theater. We acquired new Puerto Rican friends.

Soon after arriving in New York, we were reunited with Rev. and Mrs. Kim Chong Man, living in New Jersey, with whom we had worked on Jeju Island with the ICA. Through them, we once again met Rev. Kang Byoung Hoon. In July, after a 12-year absence, I visited Korea, as the guest of ICA Korea, Rev. Kang, and Rev. Park Si Won. I was excited and impressed by the many changes in Korea—the skyscrapers, car-jammed streets, and subways. We visited the two village projects where I had lived and worked. In the Jeju village, there was a stone commemorating our service with our names carved on it. The roads had been paved, and there were modern buildings and appliances. It was wonderful being with old friends again. Most of my colleagues had gotten their doctorates from US seminaries, their dissertations based on experiences with the EI and ICA in Korea, and had large congregations. Rev. Kang was general secretary of the board of missions of the Korean Methodist Church. While I was there, I attended a village consultation that Rev. Park's church conducted in a village north of Seoul. This was a miraculous reconnection of my past with my present.

Other reconnections continued to happen. In New York, we

were excited to meet Donrad Duncan, a young man with whom we had done village development in Jamaica. He was now an international designer with Bugle Boy. We enjoyed hosting some of our Venezuelan colleagues in our apartment as well as a few of our American friends and colleagues. One day, Barbara Bailey, the former mayor of Indiahoma called us to say hello. It was great to be back in touch after nine years. My dear mother paid us a visit in New York, her first time to be in the Big Apple. It was also good to reconnect with my brother, Duncan, and his family who lived down the corridor near Washington, D.C.

I was conducting a job search campaign in 15 different categories of work with several versions of my CV tailored to different jobs. My appointment with Dr. G. Shabbir Cheema of UNDP was on September 19. That was my doorway into the UN as a consultant and later a staff member. I owe my UN career to Shabbir to whom I am deeply grateful.

14

UNDP URBAN MANAGEMENT PROGRAM (UMP): New York City; New Rochelle, NY; and planet Earth

Christopher attended a Christian Brothers School, La Salle Academy. Benjamin was a freshman on scholarship at University of California at Santa Barbara. Mary worked with the Mega-Cities Project, and I had a full-time consulting contract with the United Nations Development Program (UNDP) monitoring the Urban Management Program with activities in Asia, Africa, and Latin America. UNDP was the coordinator of the system of UN agencies such as UNICEF, UNESCO, and FAO, and had just published the first Human Development Report. When I had interviewed with Shabbir Cheema, I mentioned that the nonprofit I had been with for 22 years referred to our work as "human development." I felt as though I could contribute something to UNDP. I was pleased to be working with a Pakistani American urban development expert, Dr. Cheema, and with a Dutch administrator, Frank Hartvelt. It was exciting to work at the United Nations, feeling connected to the whole planet. When I was in elementary school, I had read in our civics newspaper about this organization that represented and cared for the whole world and had been touched by this. Also, when I was in Jamaica, I had a vision that one day I would work with the UN. Now I was part of it on the development side. Of course, the UN with 193 member states, also included bodies for international dialogue and deliberation such as the General Assembly and the Security Council.

United Nations Headquarters, NYC

At the end of 1990, I prepared a paper "Human Development and Urbanization" for an international think tank on Whole Systems Transformation led by Jean Houston and held in Bocono, Venezuela. I missed not being able to attend but sent a poem and paper instead.

In April 1991, I designed and conducted a two-day seminar in Caracas, Venezuela, for the partners of an auditing/consulting firm, Krygier, Montilla y Asociados. The title of the seminar was "Orchestrating Organizational Energy with a Whole System Transition of Self, Society and Planet." Its design and content were from many sources including processes of Jean Houston and Ken Wilber. I took the participants on a mental journey from the macrocontext to microcontext of space-time, the multidimensionality of space-time, an exploration of a holistic consciousness of self, society, and planet, releasing creative energy to increase effectiveness, to the dance of musical management. With the ICA I had always worked in a team context; therefore, this was the first seminar that I designed and facilitated by myself. I was awake all of the night before the seminar, worrying. It was a kind of test to see if, after so many years of corporate work, I could do something entirely by myself. I learned that I could.

Mary and I were still struggling with where, how, when, and on what we might each focus further graduate studies. We were asking the question, What am I called to do, to know, to be? I was not sure if my story, our story, would continue to unfold or not. Only the Mystery knew. In any case, whether it was one more day or fifty years, I knew that my life had been full to overflowing. For this I experienced much gratitude. And it was out of this deep sense of gratitude that I wanted to share my story with other people.

Incredible things continued to happen to me. In August 1991, our family moved to New Rochelle, New York, a thirty-minute train ride north of Grand Central Terminal. Our move was precipitated by four factors. One was Benjamin's return home after leaving UC Santa Barbara. Benjamin hated living in New York City's East Village.

Unlike his brother, Christopher loved living in Manhattan, maybe too much. He began roaming about the city with his friends. One night he was with some friends in a park making some noise, and the police showed up and pulled guns on them. It was not a grave misdeed, but it could have been tragic, if the police had been overly anxious or careless. Christopher needed another, calmer environment in which to complete his high school career.

Mary was going through a few struggles—with menopause, with a difficult work situation at the Mega Cities Project, with attempting to care for Benjamin, and in attempting to keep Christopher from harming himself as he explored his adolescence. She experienced the energy of the city as chaotic, unrelenting, and confusing, for herself and her little family. Also, the dissolution of our Order and our roles in it may have been challenging for Mary to move beyond.

The fourth factor was my job at UNDP. I wanted to identify with the lifestyle of my close colleagues who lived in the suburbs north of the city. I felt that this would place me in the energy field that would position me to be part of the culture of an international civil servant.

In the lovely city of New Rochelle on the Long Island Sound, we moved into our first-ever single-family home. After living in a community setting with other families for 23 years, it was thrilling to have our own family home. The house was spacious and comfortable, and was protected by tall oak trees, dramatic rock formations, and beautiful flowers and shrubs. We settled in and began to change our rhythm and energy level. Life became slower and calmer. We became more reflective. The tensions continued, of course, with our two sons, but there was an enabling environment.

I was ecstatic with my new life with UNDP. I felt like a citizen of the world. I traveled on missions to Nairobi, Paris, Washington, D.C., and Brussels. After so many years of being an executive director, I loved not being in charge of an organization but being a member of a team and assisting my colleagues. My work focused on the Urban Management Program (UMP), a global initiative to improve urban management in developing countries. Through this work, I became familiar with UNDP, the World Bank, and the United Nations Centre for Human Settlement (UNCHS; now UN Habitat), which were working together on the program along with several bilateral agencies, NGOs, countries, and cities.

In Nairobi and Washington, D.C., I conducted an assessment of the first five years of the UMP and wrote a report on my findings, an "Internal Review of the Impact of the UNDP/World Bank, UNCHS Urban Management Program: 1986-1991." I wrote several papers, including "Access to Basic Urban Services in Low Income Settlements in Developing Countries." I also helped Shabbir publish two books for UNDP on an urban development cooperation strategy, *Cities, People, and Poverty*, and urban environmental improvement, *The Urban Environment.*

15

UNDP LOCAL INITIATIVE FACILITY FOR THE URBAN ENVIRONMENT (LIFE), AND FATHER-IN-LAW'S PASSING: Larchmont, NY; Peekskill, NY; New York City; Planet Earth

In 1992, after two years as a full-time consultant, I was asked to become a UNDP senior technical adviser. It meant a lot to me to have a UN passport, a *laissez passer*. I was now an international civil servant and felt like a world citizen. I was asked to design and coordinate a global program on the urban environment—the Local Initiative Facility for Urban Environment (LIFE). Dr. Cheema and I designed the LIFE program in consultation with mayors, nongovernmental organization (NGO) networks, cities' associations and bilateral donor agencies. In designing, I made use of my ICA community development experience. The program was launched at the Earth Summit in Rio de Janeiro, Brazil, in May 1992.

Mary and I had been renting the house in New Rochelle. When the owner wanted to put it on the market, we decided to move rather than make an offer. Mary found a top-floor apartment in Albee Court (where the writer Edward Albee had lived) in nearby Larchmont. From there, we could walk to the beautiful Long Island Sound, and I could take the Metro-North Railroad into Manhattan. The apartment had an outdoor patio on the roof of the building, which we enjoyed. This building is where Christopher met Jennifer. She was 16 and lived in the building for which her mother, Kathy, was superintendent. Christopher and Jennifer went to Mamaroneck High School and later college together. Mary and I loved Jennifer and thought that she and Christopher were good for each other.

Family in Larchmont, New York: left to right – Matthew, Lisa,
Duncan, Benjamin, Mary, Jennifer, Dad, Mother, Christopher, me

From my journal:

September 15, 1992:

NYC's Grand Central Terminal. The Great Hall at Grand Central is the location of an intricate social dance of human bodies streaming across its floor from every direction at every angle, crisscrossing, intersecting, but amazingly without collisions. Everyone is walking in environmental awareness of everyone around them, adjusting speed, angle, direction, in subtle ways to allow for this beautiful dance. Phillip Glass's "Glass Pieces" has captured this wonderfully in one of its dances. This social dance is living proof that people are willing to give each other the space to be, to celebrate a world together, to create a dance together.

September 16, 1992:

The yellow rose has opened its soft fluted petals welcoming me to my office.

Commuting. The contrasts: glass and steel canyons and tree-lined lawns, flowers, and single-family houses, connected by a train, back and forth, a flow inward to the center and a flow outward to the edge, a breathing in and out, an attraction to-and-fro, a pulsing, an organism. The city is alive, 20,000,000 souls flowing like blood cells to different parts of the body.

Rushing calmly, serenely, a mode of intensity and detachment. The background is anxious serenity.

The Secretary-General walked solemnly with the guards who placed a wreath on his predecessor's memorial—a ceremony of commitment and service to the planet.

I enjoy walking across the street from UNDP to the UN after lunch and taking a coffee, then mingling with the delegates, then the tourists. The human contact outside the work environment is invigorating.

We are entrusted with the responsibility to travel around the world, making decisions about millions of dollars of development initiatives. How to genuinely be of service—presence, action, thought—in every way?

Over the next two years, I initiated the LIFE program in eight countries—Pakistan, Thailand, Tanzania, Senegal, Egypt, Morocco, Jamaica and Brazil. The objective of the program was to promote "local-local" dialogue to improve the urban environment. The LIFE process in each country included three stages: 1) upstream—establishing the national program infrastructure; 2) downstream—funding and implementing small scale projects; and 3) upstream—documenting and sharing the lessons learned for policy dialogue. I spent about one week per country launching the national program. In that timeframe, I visited people identified by the UNDP country office who might be involved in establishing a national LIFE program. These were mayors, national government officials, NGO officials, low-income community leaders, donors, and a few private company representatives. We then invited a selection of those we had visited to the UNDP country office to design and initiate the program for that country.

My first LIFE mission was to Bangkok, Thailand, in October 1992. I held individual meetings with 26 people during the week and then convened a group meeting at the end of the week with selected representatives to form the LIFE national steering committee. It was amazing what could be accomplished in one week.

The small-scale LIFE projects included improving sanitation, solid waste collection, water and air quality, environmental health, and environmental education. Each country program had a talented national coordinator and a committed national selection committee and provided funds for selected small-scale projects based on proposals submitted by NGOs, community-based organizations (CBOs) and local governments. These projects included, for example, canal rehabilitation in Thailand, solid waste collection in Egypt, paper recycling in Brazil, low-cost sanitation in Pakistan, water supply in Jamaica, tree planting in Senegal, and street kids vocational training in Tanzania. While focusing on these concrete tasks of improving living conditions in low-income settlements, LIFE promoted collaboration among the local actors, CBOs, NGOs, and local authorities. LIFE also funded regional and global projects designed and implemented by international NGOs like Habitat International to document successful urban environmental initiatives. Later I made monitoring missions back to Thailand and Jamaica.

LIFE National Coordinators: Back row, left to right: Emad Adly, Egypt; Bachir Gaye, Senegal; Bakyt Beshimov, Kyrgyzstan; Sompong Patpui, Thailand; Marcia Hextall, Jamaica; Fayyaz Baquir, Pakistan; me (Global Coordinator) Front row, left to right: Marcela Marcimino, UN Office of Project Services; Mary Kibogoya, Tanzania; Brigitte Kheir, Lebanon; Ricardo Neves, Brazil; Zaida Salas Franco, Colombia

Also during the next two years, I spoke on urban development at international conferences in Fez, Morocco; Lisbon, Portugal; Paris; Vancouver; Stockholm; San Francisco; Ottawa; Washington, D.C.; Geneva; and Kuala Lumpur, Malaysia. I wrote several papers, including "Human Development into the 21ˢᵗ Century," "Report on Eight Missions Initiating LIFE," "The First Year of Local-Local Dialogue," and "Report of the LIFE Global Advisory Committee Workshop."

I was able to utilize consultants in the LIFE program who were trained in ICA's Technology of Participation (ToP) methods. They facilitated national and international workshops in Stockholm; Suez, Egypt; and Rio de Janeiro. The consultants included Jan Sanders, who helped me with a workshop in New York City for the national coordinators and became one of my top consultants.

During those two years, my family members continued to evolve. Mary was studying for a master's degree in family and pastoral counseling at Iona College, a Christian Brothers school, in New Rochelle. She enjoyed working with her clients. She was the group processor in the Guild for Spiritual Guidance at Wainwright House, an alternative educational center in Rye, New York, for which I served on the board of trustees. Mary was also on the board of directors of ICARE, an NGO providing housing for homeless people in Larchmont.

Benjamin received an associate degree in business and accounting from the State University of New York (SUNY) at Canton. He had a 3.85 GPA, of which we were all proud. He then transferred to Pace University in Pleasantville, New York, where he studied for and received his BS in business and accounting.

Christopher graduated from high school and was thinking about what to do next. He was not eager to rush into university, although his parents preferred that he do just that. He enjoyed his music and his friends. Later he did study at State University of New York Purchase and graduated with a BA in Spanish.

After many years of being an aficionado of the dance, watching dance performances of all sorts around the world, I joined a beginners ballet class at the SUNY Purchase conservatory. To get ready, I increased my workouts in the local gym. I was so nervous about joining that Mary kindly drove me to my first lesson. I was the oldest student and one of only two men. I enjoyed practicing for nine months this classical Western art form with all of its discipline and seeking perfection of form and transcendence of earthly existence. I also enjoyed practicing zazen with a group in Rye, meeting in the Quaker House.

I made a presentation on UNDP's urban strategy at the global Habitat conference of the UN Centre for Human Settlements (UNCHS), held in Vancouver, Canada. And I made a presentation on UNDP's urban agriculture project, at the International Development Research Center's (IDRC) global workshop, in Montreal, Canada.

In 1994, I helped Shabbir Cheema design and host the International Colloquium of Mayors for Social Development at the UN. This was the first time that delegates sat in the General Assembly behind names of cities rather than nations, the UN being a collectivity of nation states. We had to get special permission from the UN to do this. Hazel Henderson, author of *The Politics of the Solar Age,* spoke at my invitation. The colloquium was a great success.

I also conducted monitoring missions back to Senegal, Tanzania, and Thailand to strengthen the LIFE Program, and a mission to India to provide technical assistance for the launch of the UNCHS Sustainable Cities Program in Madras, India. I made a presentation on UNDP's urban strategy at the International Conference of Mayors in Lisbon. I also made a presentation on UNDP's urban strategy and experience at the UNICEF global conference of mayors, in Mexico City. My frequent coughing during my talk caused Jim Grant, the head of UNICEF to comment that he was concerned about the sustainability of my presentation as I discussed sustainable urban development. I designed and facilitated a global advisory committee meeting of LIFE in

Stockholm—attended by the LIFE national coordinators, bilateral donors, international NGOs—as well as an international workshop on participatory local governance in New York. Gus Edgren, the head of UNDP's policy bureau, who attended the meeting, said "I am glad finally to know the meaning of life (LIFE)."

On May 11, 1994, as I finished the draft of the first 50 years of my autobiography, I asked myself, what next? This is what I wrote: "I would like to continue my work with UNDP for several more years. Through this work I will assist developing countries to formulate policies, programs, and projects of social equity and ecological harmony in local urban communities and organizations. I would also like to contribute to UNDP's evolving understanding of sustainable human development (SHD).

"I would like to deepen and expand my learning in a doctoral program on whole systems urban development with the graduate school of the Union Institute. This process will make my contribution through UNDP and beyond more effective.

"I want to continue my ballet lessons and to learn modern dance and choreography. This activity will stimulate my personal creativity and delight in rhythm, movement, form, and design.

"I want to continue helping the members of my little family to develop and realize their full potential. This activity will ground me in intimate relationships of care.

"After I leave UNDP, I want to use my skills to consult with organizations and communities, to do more writing and to offer seminars on personal and social transformation.

"This July 31, I will celebrate my fiftieth birthday and meditate on the rest of my life. A few days later we will move, one more time, this time to Peekskill, a small city on the east bank of the Hudson River. We chose this town of 19,000 for several reasons. Peekskill is a mixture of people—poor, middle class and wealthy, of African Americans, Hispanics, Caucasians and Asian Americans. It is becoming an artists' community. It is in the beautiful wooded hills of the Hudson River Valley in northern Westchester County, an hour train ride from Manhattan's Grand Central Terminal. We found a house there which we could afford without stretching to the limit, with the help of Mary's dad, and where we can create a home and a place for writing, thinking, dialogue, and celebration with our family and friends.

"This story of a social artist continues . . ."

In 1994, I did celebrate my 50th birthday. My mother gave me a photo album from birth to marriage, such a thoughtful, loving gift. We did move to Peekskill. Christopher graduated from high school in Mamaroneck. Benjamin graduated from SUNY and entered Pace University. Mary was in the final year of her master's. But I decided that I was too busy with my work to pursue a doctorate.

In 1995, I made a presentation on UNDP's urban development experience at a Rotary International global workshop in San Francisco. There I met Dr. Harold Nelson, a professor of whole system design, who is still my friend, and Hazel Henderson. Later I enjoyed speaking to one of Harold's whole system design classes at Antioch University Seattle.

Also that year, I made a keynote on UNDP's experience in historic cities and development at UNESCO Historic Cities Conference, in Fez, Morocco. The old city of Fez was fascinating, so many winding narrow little stone streets.

I conducted initiating missions to South Africa, Kyrgyzstan, Colombia, and Bangladesh to establish LIFE in each country. There were now 12 pilot countries with projects improving living conditions in slums in 60 cities. And I designed and facilitated the annual retreats of the management and governance division and the social equity and poverty reduction division both in the policy bureau in New York. My facilitation skills were well received, and this began my role as an in-house facilitator for UNDP, even though I had been hired as a local governance policy adviser. I enjoyed serving my colleagues in this way.

For four months, Mary had not been feeling well and had

gone for a checkup. Her doctor discovered ovarian cancer. I was devastated and was afraid of losing her. In March 1995, Mary had surgery to remove the cancer and her ovaries. The wait during her surgery was frightening for me even though her surgeon at Columbia Presbyterian Hospital was excellent. After the operation, he told us that he got all of the tumor and that Mary would not need follow-up chemotherapy. Our family was shaken by all of this. Mary was for her family and friends a pillar of strength, wisdom, and kindness.

It was hard to focus on my work after Mary's illness. However, I did continue, and designed and facilitated a global advisory committee meeting of LIFE in Cairo, Egypt. Fortunately, Mary had recovered enough from her surgery that she was able to go with me; so, our family bought her a ticket. After the meeting, we visited the pyramids and other sites.

Participating in regular Mystery Schools with Jean Houston continued to enliven Mary and me in our life and work. Being able to be with many different kinds of people, to dance, to dialogue, to dream, to engage in psycho-physical exercises, to hear Jean's powerful lectures, and to be in beautiful nature were all life giving to a UN policy adviser. It was also meaningful to be in Mystery School with ICA colleagues such as Jan Sanders and Charlene Powell. We sometimes got lost driving from New York City to the Greenkill Retreat Center in Huguenot, New York, and laughed about this as being part of the mystery.

On July 31, my birthday, I wrote in my journal: *"I have decided that I do not want to be a bureaucrat for the rest of my life. I want to write, to teach, to consult, to create, to dance, to transform, to inspire, to enthuse. God help me in my work—to prioritize, to be productive, to be detached, to be compassionate, to be creative, to take risks, to enable the system, to be my being, to know my knowing, and to do my doing. God help me to be, fully, in bliss, in ecstasy, in acceptance, in love, in transformative relationship to all that I encounter."*

In October, my parents visited us in our Peekskill home. After celebrating my dad's 80th birthday, I flew to Berlin, Germany, to chair the Urban Management Program Donor Workshop and make a presentation at a global conference on urban development. The evening before my presentation I ate steak, drank wine, and had a very sweet dessert. I went to bed anxious about my presentation the next morning. I awoke at 2:30 a.m. with a feeling of banging in my chest. It felt like a live chicken was jumping around in my rib cage. I was frightened and had no idea what was happening. After a while, I went out in the hallway and looked for anyone who was awake at that hour. Someone was, and he told me that the Humboldt Hospital was nearby the Villa Borsig, where we were staying and meeting. He took me there by taxi.

The doctors tried various medications, but nothing worked to return my heart to its regular rhythm. Finally, the doctors decided to give me electric shock. They made me unconscious and shocked me with a paddle. When I woke up, they told me my heart was back in rhythm. This began my journey with atrial fibrillation (AFib). After the first episode, I felt that perhaps I was not living the life that I should. Perhaps I had too much stress flying around the world so often. I stopped taking caffeinated and alcoholic drinks and stopped eating beef, pork and excessive sugar. But I kept my stressful life and work, meditated, and survived, flourished, and kept having AFib. What was going on that Mary and I both had serious health challenges just a few months apart? Was it that time in life when mortality reminds you again that it is here?

In November, I realized clearly that UNDP was my current vehicle to pursue my calling of helping people achieve their full potential. Over the years, there were many days I wanted to leave UNDP. Other days I wanted to stay and do all that I could in and through the organization. It was back and forth.

I wrote in my journal in December that I wanted to be a "chaplain" of sorts in UNDP. What did I mean by that? I realized that I wanted to be there for my colleagues, to sometimes help them understand in a deep way what is going on in the world and in their own lives and to enable them to be more effective, happier, and more self-giving. This meant that I would sometimes introduce theological, philosophical, and depth-psychological insights and processes into my work at UNDP. I realized that doing this would make use of my academic education in theology and literature along with my professional training in community, organizational, and leadership development. Of course, often I would fail to care for others, and I needed to continue practicing staying in touch with my own heart especially in the midst of so much travel and so many activities. Many times my colleagues exercised care for me for which I was grateful.

In 1996 in Paris, I made a presentation on UNDP's governance policy at the Organization for Economic Co-operation and Development (OECD) Development Assistance Committee (DAC) Task Force on Participatory Development and Good Governance. (Such long names!) After the meeting, I walked around central Paris taking in the ambience of the River Seine, Arc de Triomphe, Catedral de Notre Dame, traffic sounds, smells of freshly baked bread, and tastes of French food. Often I felt so lucky to be able to travel and be with people of other cultures.

That year I provided technical advice in the UNDP country offices in Tanzania, Thailand, and India on decentralization and local governance programs. Also during this period, I designed the second phase of the UMP and arranged a donor consultation. I conducted evaluations of LIFE for phases I and II, designed phase III, and recruited a new global coordinator, Dr. Pratibha Mehta from India. (She is now head of UNDP in Tajikistan and previously in Vietnam and Yemen.) I wrote a concept paper on the design of phase III of the UMP. I coordinated along with Jack Smit and Jonas Rabinovitch an Urban Agriculture Project and helped prepare a groundbreaking publication on the findings, *Urban Agriculture: Food, Jobs, and Sustainable Cities.*

I raised $12 million for the LIFE Program from bilateral

donors, including Sweden, Germany, and Norway. I enjoyed designing and facilitating annual retreats for the Management Development and Governance Division of UNDP, of which I was part, and also the Social Equity and Poverty Eradication Division both in the Bureau of Development Policy (BDP). I also designed and facilitated a global workshop in the Asian Ministerial Conference on Governance held in Lahore, Pakistan, a global advisory committee meeting of LIFE in Istanbul, Turkey, and a global workshop in New York to brainstorm UNDP's policy on governance.

In 1996, my father-in-law, Ben Avery, learned that the cancer in his jaw had returned. Mary flew out to Phoenix to be with him. After an earlier surgery, he had continued to do pushups every morning in his 80s and climb Squaw Peak in Phoenix. Part of his jaw had been removed, and his food had to be blended. One day he said, "Life just isn't fun anymore." So, he got a Zane Grey novel, lay on his bed reading, and stopped eating. His grandkids would visit and sit on his bed. Hearing Mary talk about this on the phone touched me deeply. Several days later, he died on May 8. I flew out to Phoenix and accompanied Mary and her sister Marjorie Bachert to view his body. What a great man he was. He had helped create the Phoenix Mountain park system. He had been a reporter with a major Arizona newspaper and a member of the Western Regional Parks Board for the National Park Service. After the memorial service, Christopher and his mother drove back to New York, bringing some special family items from her parents' home.

Before he passed away, a shooting range near Phoenix that he and his sporting club had built in the 1950s and 1960s was named after him. He had taught his youngest daughter, Mary, how to shoot when she was a girl, and she had become one of the top US national women's rifle champions. She could hit a bull's-eye on a misty, windy day. I kidded her that I would never irritate her too much for that reason.

His granddaughter Rebecca Bentley, great-granddaughter Brenda and great-grandson Lane still live in Arizona.

That year Benjamin graduated from Pace University in Pleasantville, New York, with a bachelor's in business and accounting. We were so proud of him. Sometimes he would mention to us that he wanted to start his own restaurant. Over the years since his graduation, he worked in retail as a successful and well-respected manager north of New York City. We loved to eat together in nearby Korean restaurants.

In May, Mary lovingly gave me a French horn, and I began playing again. I was so happy. I loved the mellow sound, the round brass tubing, and playing classical Western music. It was not an easy instrument, and I had not played since high school. I got a good local teacher who helped me. I was thrilled to play pieces by Mozart, Strauss, Haydn, Brahms, Beethoven, and others.

In August, my dad had a mild heart attack damaging 10 to 20 percent of the wall of his upper heart. I flew to Oklahoma to be with mom and dad, and Duncan arrived soon after. Mom and then dad became emotional as it began to sink in that their routine had been broken. I tried to make them comfortable and feel secure. I assured them that I and all their family loved them and would take care of them. It felt strange that my dad who had always been such a strong man was now so vulnerable. I realized that mortality was all of our destiny. Fortunately, he recovered shortly and resumed much of his previous schedule.

Back in New York, I designed and facilitated a global workshop to help create UNDP's first corporate policy on governance and contributed to and helped publish the first-ever UNDP policy paper on "Governance for Sustainable Human Development: Official Policy Paper." It was wonderful to use ICA strategic planning methods in the workshop. Held at UN headquarters, people came from around the world to participate, from national and local governments, national and regional NGOs, bilateral and multilateral donors, UNDP country offices and headquarters, and others. Participants brainstormed and agreed on a five-year policy vision, current obstacles to that vision, and strategic policy directions. Henning Karcher, a senior UNDP HQ official told me later that it was the best workshop he had experienced.

In November, I traveled to Seoul, Bangkok, Lahore, and Delhi. In Bangkok, I visited two districts and two slum projects supported by LIFE, and rode in a boat through a polluted canal. I also met with the LIFE National Taskforce, the UN Resident Coordinator, the governor's team, and subcontractors. They agreed that LIFE was a model for the Bangkok Metropolitan Authority's partnership work. Later, I meditated in two temples. At one point the temple dogs surrounded me barking.

In December, I traveled to Dar es Salaam, Tanzania, After a seven hour flight to Zurich and a short rest, I flew another nine hours to Dar on the Indian Ocean. Before my first appointment, I bent my glasses frame and went to a shop to fix them. From my many meetings, I felt that growth, equity, and education might be even more important for the country than decentralization. I also realized that the country needed a series of forums at all levels to create "buy in" in the implementation of the local government reform agenda. It was hot and humid, and I wondered if it was snowing in New York.

I began to appreciate that perhaps I had "earned a kind of UNDP PhD" in urban development and decentralization. My mentor and boss, Dr. G. Shabbir Cheema, was a world-renowned urban scholar. I had read vast amounts of literature on the topics. I had written several technical papers and helped publish a few books on these subjects. I was applying my learning by designing new programs and advising cities and countries on their urban policies. All of this was building on my previous experiences of community development in several countries. Well, in any case, I was grateful for all that I had learned and done in this phase of my life.

16

UNDP DECENTRALIZED GOVERNANCE, AND MOTHER-IN-LAW'S PASSING: New York City; Peekskill, NY; and planet Earth

In 1997, UNDP promoted me on an accelerated basis to the D1 (director) level, and I became principal technical adviser for decentralized governance. Leading the global team on decentralization and local governance included designing, launching, and coordinating the Decentralized Governance Program. I provided technical advice to the UNDP country offices in Uganda and the Philippines on the design of programs in local governance and decentralization.

In January, I traveled to Jamaica, and facilitated a global workshop of LIFE coordinators in Kingston, Jamaica. It was meaningful to be back again in Jamaica, where I had lived and worked with the ICA in the Blue Mountains and Kingston, doing community and organizational development. After the workshop, I was able to visit the village of Woburn Lawn and meet former ICA staff and volunteers, including Winston Davis, and Woburn Lawn leaders, including Alice Wright and Anabel Crosdale.

After Jamaica, I flew to Tulsa, Oklahoma, and attended an International Association of Facilitators (IAF) conference, and then visited my parents in Durant. I realized that my parents were getting older and may need special care sooner than later. I played two "concerts" for them on my French horn; and Mary and I held a workshop to help them think about their future vision and plans. It was very intense.

I enjoyed leading a global research project on decentralized governance with our partner, MIT in Cambridge, Massachusetts, and ten national research institutes in five regions of the world, resulting in the dissemination of case studies and a synthesis on the UNDP website. The topic of the research was the role of participation in service delivery to the poor. For research interchange, the national researchers from the ten countries, Professor Paul Smoke of MIT, and I held a meeting in Amman, Jordan, to discuss our findings. The final paper was prepared by Professor Smoke, Dr. Jan Loubser, George Walters, Mounir Tabet and Elena Marcelino, with myself as chief editor. Later it was published in a book edited by Shabbir Cheema and Dennis Rondinelli, *Reinventing Government for the Twenty-first Century: State Capacity in a Globalizing Society.*

A typical day for me when I was home and in the office looked like this: I woke up at 6 a.m., then sat on my floor cushion and meditated, took a hot shower, ate breakfast of yogurt, berries, and nuts, drove five minutes to the tiny train stop down by the Hudson, waited for the train, climbed up and boarded, found a seat, traveled southward along the river for one hour, arrived at Grand Central, walked east ten minutes to the UN on the East River, went through security into the building, took the elevator up to my floor, walked into my office, said hello to Josie Catuncan, my support staff, and other colleagues, started my computer, answered emails from the LIFE coordinators, welcomed UNDP resident representatives from various countries and other guests for appointments, did some writing on a policy paper, made phone calls to bilateral donors, attended in-house meetings, designed new projects, facilitated a meeting, arranged my next overseas mission reservations, walked across the street to the UN cafeteria for lunch with a colleague, maybe Mounir Tabet, Charles McNeill, Nikhil Chandavarkar, or Cosmas Gitta, stopped by the Dag Hammarskjold meditation room in the UN to sit quietly, returned to my office, continued sending and reading emails, made more calls, held additional appointments and meetings, wrote some more, looked out the windows, turned off my computer, said goodbye to colleagues, walked to Grand Central, caught the train northbound, viewed the mighty river and the fascinating people on the train, reflected, got off in the bird sanctuary near my home, drove to my house, greeted family members, fixed and ate dinner, talked with my wife, reflected, read, prepared for bed, and fell asleep. Gratitude.

In April, I traveled to Kampala, Uganda. The airport on Lake Victoria was orderly and efficient. Driving on rough roads into the capitol, we saw many huts and people selling clay pots. It was warm and sunny with great cloud formations piling up. Huge cranes circled overhead. One large old crane was eating butterflies, its big beak snapping at the insects. I was aware that my lower front four teeth had become crooked whereas they used to be straight. I realized that I was an animal, growing old, my crooked beak snapping at the fleetingness of life. While there, I worked with the UNDP office to improve the design of the decentralized governance program. After that we visited a local district. Everyone I met impressed me. I wrote in my journal that evening: "I am at peace – still conscious of my heart – but at peace. Life – what a supreme mystery!"

Back in New York City, I produced and disseminated on the UNDP website a monograph on good experiences of decentralized governance from all regions. I established an electronic discussion group on decentralized governance for donors. I helped prepare and publish the book *Reconceptualizing Governance*. That year I also mobilized $1 million in cost sharing from mostly European donors for UNDP urban projects.

Based on a global evaluation of LIFE, I prepared and disseminated worldwide the book *Participatory Local Governance: Analysis of Experience and Methodology of the LIFE Program 1992-1997.*

In May, I traveled to Manila by way of Tokyo, becoming aware of flying over the north pole at 882 miles per hour. My mission was to support a governance workshop, help with program planning, and learn from the Philippines. My concern was to help UNDP focus on tangible assistance to the poor. It had been around twenty-four years since I was last in that country. At that time I helped conduct a regional training program at Ateneo de Manila. While there this time, I met a former ICA colleague, Dr. Kenneth Ellison, living in Manila. He was as passionate and self-confident about his life and work as ever. From my work there, I realized that UNDP needed ToP training. After our workshop we visited an urban slum. On my last night in Manila, I saw "A Dangerous Life", a movie about the assassination of Ninoy Aquino and the EDSA Revolution that followed. I was filled with emotion at the suffering of the Filipino people under Marcos and the courage and faith of Cori Aquino in running for president.

Donda Avery, Mary's mother, passed away that year. After struggling for some time with several ailments, she decided that she didn't want further medical treatment. Mary flew to Phoenix to help with arrangements along with her sister Marjorie. I went out for the memorial service. Mary was very generous with the money that her parents left her, giving gifts to our sons, my brother, her nephew, and others.

In January 1998, I designed and facilitated a staff retreat for our division at headquarters. In reflection, I realized that future retreats should have a design team, external and internal facilitators, clarification of Ken Wilber's quadrant framework, and that I should see myself as a choreographer of organizational deepening, broadening, weaving, and creating breakthroughs. In broader terms, I realized that I wanted to create in different voices, levels, and media – conceptual, poetic, musical, dance, video, emotional, and physical. The intention that I felt was to help catalyze another reinvention of society. Sometimes self-doubt wracked my being. My spiritual practice helped this doubt to be acknowledged, cared for, and dispersed to some degree.

In February, Mary and I drove from New York to Oklahoma. It was a kind of pilgrimage. We first stopped in Maryland and saw my brother Duncan and family; then we drove to Tennessee and saw Mary's nephew Scott and family. We traveled on to Hot Springs, Arkansas, and bathed in the healing waters. Next we drove to Dallas and picked up Benjamin who had flown out to join us. When we arrived in Durant, we found mother and dad in good shape. They had decided to move to Edmond to the Oklahoma Christian Home. Mary and I helped them build a ten week timeline for their move. They named it "Our New Adventure." Mary stayed to help them pack until she went to Arizona to go through the Grand Canyon.

Before I returned to New York, Mary and I discussed a possibility of moving to Oklahoma. We visited two beautiful pieces of land, both over 20 acres with houses on them, near Guthrie, Oklahoma. We had a vision of establishing an institute in Oklahoma near my parents. We seriously considered it, developing scenarios, budgets, and timelines. Our vision was that the institute would be local and global, residential and a network, profitable and benevolent, provide an ambience for meditation and reflection, celebration and art, and a demonstration of how any family can be its being in service and support itself by doing so. But, we didn't make a decision.

Mary then trekked through the Grand Canyon with her sister Marjorie. She prepared to do this while helping my parents pack. She walked up and down stadium stairs to build stamina. She and Marjorie made it down to the bottom of the canyon and back up safely! It snowed during their trip. At the bottom of the canyon, she ran into an old ICA colleague, Claudia Cramer, who gave her a quilt that she had made.

In March, I traveled from New York to Tokyo across the North Pole and the Pacific for over 13 hours. When I arrived very tired at the training center, I had chicken curry, took a hot bath, and got ready for bed. I was struck by the local neighborhood – clean, quiet, modern, yet traditional. How could Tokyo be so huge, busy, and polluted, and yet have quiet little neighborhoods like this one? The next morning I gave the keynote address at a global workshop on decentralization and local development sponsored by the Japanese International Cooperation Agency (JICA). My talk, "Decentralization, Local Governance, and Sustainable Human Development," was later published in a book by JICA. When I returned to headquarters, I designed and facilitated a retreat for UNDP's policy bureau and another workshop on pilot testing.

With all of the travel I had been doing I was becoming very familiar with itineraries, airports, airplanes, and hotels. Flying around the world had become like taking a bus ride across a city. Even jetlag was beginning to weaken. In fact, even though some would see my life as special since it was related to the UN and international development, it was really very similar to many people's experiences of family, work and personal awareness.

In April, I returned to Oklahoma to help with my parents move, explore the Oklahoma ranch scenario, celebrate Easter as a family, honor the Durant home and ritualize "letting go", thank our ancestors by visiting their graves, celebrate my parents' 55th anniversary, and then drive back to New York with Mary. She had found a new property of twenty-eight acres near Lawton, Oklahoma, and the Wichita Mountains. We went to see it, found it intriguing, and continued getting advice and building scenarios. It was a fascinating prospect, but I had mixed feelings about it. Mary was more excited to live in the country "out west." After more analysis and discussion over the following several weeks,

Mary said that we shouldn't move to Oklahoma. Was she sensing my reluctance? Was this more my decision to which she gave her gracious support? Did she do that often? Did I do it also? I was grateful for our partnership, but was I as supportive of her dreams as she was of mine?

In June, I travelled to Stockholm, Sweden, and Amman, Jordan. A light rain was falling when I arrived in Stockholm. Even though very tired, I prepared for the next day's workshop with donors which I wanted to be a humanizing event, not a typical bureaucratic meeting. Amman was full of bright light, a white stone city. Preparing for the research workshop, I realized that I must set aside ego to enable the group to be intellectually honest, non-defensive, open, clear, and creative. One early morning, I went into AFib twice, but returned to sinus rhythm through meditation. I found myself thinking about the beautiful property in Oklahoma, early retirement, traveling less, meditating more, being with my parents, and doing only work in which I completely believed.

In July, for my self-care and spiritual development, I attended a retreat at Holy Cross Monastery on the Hudson.

In August, I visited mother and dad in Edmond. They seemed to be doing well. When I returned to New York, I began reading Thich Nhat Hanh's wonderful book, *The Heart of the Buddha's Teaching*. I took some time off from work, and played my horn, walked, read, did financial planning, visioning, meditating, and gardening. I was still calculating and dreaming concerning when I should retire from UNDP, do a PhD, move to Oklahoma, or form an institute. I was thinking that our institute would focus on epistemology, consciousness, social justice, connecting inner and outer, cultivating happiness and peace, practicing compassion and wisdom, art and music, culture, and spirituality. Our activities would include writing, teaching, consulting, and facilitation.

I traveled twice to Washington, D.C., once, to the World Bank, and again, to hear the profound teachings of His Holiness the XIV Dalai Lama. Much gratitude.

I flew to Nagoya, Japan, and gave a keynote at a global conference on decentralization arranged by the UN Center for Regional Development (UNCRD). I tried to inject some new images, styles, and models, and identify lessons and challenges.

Mary and I attended an introductory weekend Zen retreat at Zen Mountain Monastery (ZMM) in the Catskill Mountains of New York. The vice abbess of the monastery, even though she wasn't at ZMM that weekend, would appear later in my life in a highly significant manner.

17

UNDP MANAGEMENT DEVELOPMENT AND GOVERNANCE, DECENTRALIZED GOVERNANCE, 9/11, AND MY DAD's PASSING: New York City; Garrison, NY; and planet Earth

In 1999, I became deputy director of the Management Development and Governance Division (MDGD) and principal adviser for decentralized governance. Working with the director, Dr. Cheema, was truly a pleasure and an honor. He was not only an outstanding scholar but an effective manager who truly cared about his staff.

I traveled to Manila to attend and speak at a global workshop on decentralization and local governance, at the World Conference on Governance. When I walked out of the airport, the humidity and heat hit me in the face. In speaking at the conference, I tried to be personable, honor many people, and inject a bit of humor. In the leadership seminar chaired by former Filipino president

Ramos, I attempted to create greater self-consciousness of the group. In the workshop on decentralized governance, I tried to demonstrate how a UN official can be a facilitator who can enable a group and listen carefully to others. It was good to be there with Shabbir Cheema and Samina Kamal. After the event, I met former ICA colleague Gary Forbes who was conducting facilitator training for the Civil Service Commission. My presentation was later published in a book by the workshop sponsor. The UN helped prepare many books and papers that shared knowledge on various topics with every country.

Occasionally, I found myself asking – what does it look like to be a servant of six billion people? How can humanity wake up to clear mind, and compassionate heart? How do we awaken to our Buddha-nature? I realized that I was one of many servants of that awakening.

That year I also led the team on decentralization and local governance, coordinated the global Decentralized Governance Program, and prepared a framework and methodology on decentralized governance for country offices and an electronic discussion group.

Working with colleagues from 193 countries was a great gift and challenge. To accomplish anything took the effort of many people – support staff at headquarters, assistance from country offices, and colleagues in donor agencies, local communities, nonprofits, government – both local and national, and other international agencies.

I also conducted in-depth thematic assessments on decentralized governance in three countries—Malawi, Nepal, and Venezuela, helped prepare UNDP official publications on capacity development, and raised $2 million from European bilateral donors for UNDP urban development projects.

In June, Mary, the boys, and I moved to nearby Garrison. Mary and I had been looking at properties when we would drive up to the Catskills. Mary found a house in Garrison on Route 9D with a beautiful view of the Hudson Highlands and river, on two acres of land, one of which was wooded. We made an offer, and it was accepted. We removed old wallpaper, renovated, painted the house inside and out and moved in. Nearby, there was a tiny Metro-North train stop down by the riverbank, swamp, and bird sanctuary. That is where I would leave for Manhattan and arrive back every day. We loved that house very much and named it Hillside Cottage, and later "251." It had a double-sided fireplace, deck, and several large windows facing the Hudson. I loved taking pictures of the dramatic sunsets over the Hudson highlands from the deck. Many friends and family members visited, with many celebrations held there over the years. It was also where death and new life visited us.

On one mission, I was to fly to Amsterdam, Oslo, Berne, and London. From Amsterdam, I traveled to The Hague to chair the LIFE donor review meeting and meet with Peter de Haan to discuss support of DGIS, The Netherland's donor agency, for the Decentralized Governance Program (DGP). In Oslo, I met with NORAD, Norway's international development agency and the Ministry of Foreign Affairs regarding their support. Because of ice and fog in Oslo, I couldn't connect to Berne to meet with the Swiss. The next day, I flew to London to meet with DFID, the UK's donor agency, regarding their support of DGP at the country, regional, and global levels.

That year, Christopher graduated from the State University of New York at Purchase with a bachelor's degree in Spanish. We were so proud of him. After that event Mary said, "Well, we have launched the boys," which she also said later when both boys moved out of our house into their own apartments.

In December, I flew to Oklahoma to see mother and dad. My brother Duncan and I took turns visiting them every three months. My goals were to celebrate their being, our relationship, Christmas, and the approaching third millennium. I also bought dad a hat, helped mother with her computer, discussed their finances, arranged my next visit in March, and planned mother's visit to New York in the spring.

In 2000, my paper on "Decentralized Governance: UNDP's Experience" was published in *New Regional Development Paradigms Vol. 3* by the UN Center for Regional Development in Nagoya, Japan.

I provided technical advice in Nepal to the Association of District Development Committees on the draft thematic assessment on decentralization and local governance and met with government, nongovernmental and donor officials concerning Nepal's decentralization strategy. One highlight was meeting with village leaders on a hilltop. When I asked them through a translator what they had accomplished so far, one lady answered that she had learned to accept both joy and sorrow with equanimity. I was deeply touched. I had expected a response concerning some new village structure, but instead I received a spiritual teaching. Later on my own time, I visited Buddhist temples in Kathmandu. This was one of my several visits to Nepal.

My commute to UNDP was now the farthest ever. It had begun from Loisaida (Spanglish for "Lower East Side") in Manhattan, next from New Rochelle, Larchmont, Peekskill, and then from Garrison, always moving northward. It was now around one hour and ten minutes each way on the Metro-North train to and from Grand Central. This total of two hours and twenty minutes a day was not wasted time. It was always fascinating. Sometimes when I was especially tired, however, it seemed as if it took forever. Up and down the Hudson River in every kind of weather and season provided ample time for contemplation of nature and people. Sometimes mist rising from the river, other times blinding sunlight reflecting. Past the Bear Mountain Bridge, down the river, turning around the north of Manhattan, then across the bridge and underground after 125th Street, arriving at Grand Central. People-watching on the train was always interesting. And plenty of time to think, reflect, read, write, or rest was available. It provided a transition between home and work, village and city. Back and forth, breathing in and out, on the great estuary that was the Hudson. Grand Central was the peoples' temple, with its starry constellations on the ceiling, light streaming in, and the daily dance of commuters crisscrossing in complex chaordic patterns. From bird sanctuary to the Big Apple, with a short walk to the UN, and back again. Gratitude.

In June, Mary began coughing. After a while, she went to see Dr. Cynthia Ligenza, our primary care physician who was also a lung specialist, in Cold Spring. Dr. Ligenza took an X-ray of Mary's lungs. There were little spots throughout her lungs. Mary called me at work with the results saying, "We have had a wonderful life, Rob. We mustn't be greedy." I was devastated. It had been five years since Mary's cancer surgery. After five years, you are usually said to be cancer free. We realized that we needed to do a biopsy to see what was actually going on. The biopsy showed that Mary had what the oncologists thought was hidden breast cancer that had spread to the lungs. She began a five-month treatment of chemotherapy. She was in high spirits, and we were hopeful for her healing and living a cancer-free life. I drove Mary regularly to Columbia Presbyterian Hospital for chemo treatments. In August, her oncologist, Dr. Amy Tiersten, told us that she now thought it was adenocarcinoma and that the best-case scenario was that it was ovarian related. They continued chemo, as there was not enough tissue for hormone receptor treatment. She felt a cure was very possible. Dr. Tiersten actually wasn't certain of the source but decided that they would treat it as ovarian cancer. The surgeon who had operated five years ago had said that ovarian cancer doesn't metastasize in the lungs. What was going on? How were we going to heal Mary?

It was hard to get back to work when Mary was in danger. My awareness of her condition seemed to be always with me. And yet, I would forget for a time in order to focus on a task. But then the awareness would reappear in my chest, with its worry, and uncertainty.

In July, mom and dad came to visit us in Garrison. Duncan and his family also came; and we had a wonderful celebration of mother's birthday. Dad was getting weaker and more confused but we still had a good time being together. It was dad's last visit.

Back with UNDP, I led an international team to Kyrgyzstan that created a new decentralization national policy using participatory workshops and review mechanisms. Formerly part of the Soviet Union, Kyrgyzstan had gained its independence and had its own government. Fledgling nonprofits were beginning to appear. The mountains and lakes were so beautiful. I have a photo of me wearing a heavy coat and beret standing in a boat on an icy lake with snowy mountains in the background. How was Mary doing back home? How could I be present in my here and now, and also with her in every moment? Impossible, and yet the undercurrents of awareness and sadness were ever flowing.

In Kyrgyzstan

My dad passed away on December 3, 2000, at 4:59 p.m. He and mother had visited us in New York in July, and then he had been weakening since September, when I had visited Edmond to provide support. He was becoming more confused and was living in the rest home near mother's cottage in the retirement community in Edmond. We celebrated his birthday for the last time on October 24. Amazingly, over the previous few months, he had become sweeter and funnier and enjoyed kidding with the support staff. One day Mother called my brother Duncan and me and told us that the doctors felt dad was approaching the end. I immediately left from my workplace, went to the airport, and flew to Edmond on November 30 (and learned from Benjamin who had brought my suitcase to the airport, that Mary had broken her shoulder!) to be with dad and mother. I had been in the midst of facilitating a UNDP workshop and had to leave it in the capable hands of my colleagues Dr. Charles McNeil, Mounir Tabet, and Jan Sanders and rush to the airport. Duncan got to Edmond before me.

When I walked out of the Oklahoma City airport, I was struck being back on the prairie—flat, windy, big skies, horizon to horizon. When I arrived at the facility I was filled with emotion and sadness. I asked myself – what do I need to say to dad? He knows I love him. I know he loves me. Dad was not conscious but was somehow aware that I had entered his room. Perhaps he had been waiting for me. I told him again and again of my love for him. Duncan, his wife, Lisa, his son Matthew, Mother, and I sat in a small circle in dad's room. We meditated and shared our love for Dad. We were gathered around his bed the moment he stopped breathing. We burst into tears, and our hearts were broken. Then Duncan said, "His spirit is present!" We hugged each other, and lived that moment together fully. Love had broken the chains of death. Dad's spirit filled our hearts with love overflowing. The funeral home drove his body back to Durant, where we buried him near the graves of his mother, dad, brother, and parents. My mother's parents and grandparents were also buried there at

Highland Cemetery. He was truly a good man, a good son, brother, husband, father, and pastor. He would now be eternally in the authenticity of his eighty-five years – his faith, strength, loyalty, responsibility, humor, love, and service. I grieved hard and missed his presence so much.

Back in New York, UNDP was pleased with the 2000 LIFE global evaluation that found that the LIFE program had benefited over 6,000,000 people in low-income urban settlements directly and indirectly in cities around the world.

In January 2001, I went to Kyrgyzstan by way of Istanbul to facilitate a regional workshop for Eastern Europe and the Commonwealth of Independent States. I learned again that I love to facilitate group discussion and planning, have a spiritual as well as social mission, wanted to work more at the country level, have a mission to empower people, and love to dance.

When I returned to New York, I took Mary for medical tests and doctor visits. At home, I tried to comfort her by rubbing her aching feet and hands.

I helped improve the quality of decentralization policy components in country programs through conducting missions, preparing comments, providing consultant referrals and holding discussions with UNDP resident representatives (RRs) and deputy RRs in Iran, Ivory Coast, Burundi, Sierra Leone, Rwanda, Myanmar, Moldova and Malawi.

In March, I traveled to Johannesburg, South Africa, by way of Zurich. I was aware of flying over Italy, the Mediterranean Sea, Libya, Chad, Congo, Zimbabwe, and Zambia. In Jo-burg, I chaired a global donor meeting for the Urban Management Program. On the way back to New York, I stopped in Bonn, Germany, and met with officials of Germany's donor agency, BMZ, requesting their support for UNDP's urban development programs. Later that month in Trinidad, I made a presentation on governance at a Latin American/Caribbean meeting of UNDP Deputy RRs.

In April, I attended a seminar in San Francisco on chaordic

theory and development based on the writings of Dee Hock. I wanted to better understand the dynamics of how order can emerge from chaos and to apply it to the new global decentralization network and decentralization programs. My UNDP colleague Mounir Tabet also attended the seminar.

When I returned to New York, Mary had to go into the hospital for dehydration, nausea, and high white blood cell count. She then began to consider an alternative to chemotherapy; but we were not clear what that could be. I was sad and afraid and was practicing accepting our reality.

In May, I became intensely aware once again that life is suffering, impermanence and interdependence: My father had passed away, my mother was alone, my wife was very sick, my two sons had moved out of our house to their own apartments, my boss and friend had left UNDP for the UN, my coworker had also gone, my role had shifted, and my organization had changed. And at the center of all of this was a calm, quiet pillar of mystery that I called myself. But of course, from time to time the pillar would crumble, and collapse, and then I would once again try my best to wake up, be kind, and embrace the really real.

I got feedback that my work was making a difference improving the quality of decentralization policy components of UNDP's five regional programs through my written comments, discussions, data analysis, and providing advice for regional fora and workshops. Five headquarters units reported that they benefited from my policy advice on the HIV/AIDS-decentralization linkages.

In terms of my own life, by now, I had read nineteen books on Buddhism, attended several retreats, and was meditating daily. I was finding the philosophy and methods profound and effective. At the end of August, I attended a retreat in Garrison with the Venerable Dugu Choegyal Rimpoche. At the opening, he called us to be low key, humble, loose, light, and easy. He asked us to hold an attitude of gratitude, and light mindfulness at all times. I took lots of notes, and found it so helpful.

One September morning as usual, I took the Metro-North commuter train to Manhattan. It was a clear, summery day. Usually, I took her, but today Benjamin drove his mother to Columbia Presbyterian Hospital for her chemotherapy treatment. When I arrived at Grand Central Terminal, one of my favorite places in the world, I noticed people gathered around a TV monitor in one of the newsstands. There was an image of smoke on the screen. Someone next to me said "an airplane has accidentally hit the World Trade Center." I then walked east the four blocks to my office at UNDP and took the elevator to my floor thinking about the air crash. When I got to my office, several colleagues were crowded around a computer screen. A colleague looked up and said, "Terrorists have crashed into the World Trade Center, and we are afraid that the UN may be next." I went into my office and cried for the people dying and for the confusion and hatred of those who drove the planes into the building full of people.

Shabbir and I then went with our colleague Pratibha to her nearby apartment. From there we could see the smoke rising from the collapse of the two towers in southern Manhattan. We realized that we shouldn't stay in the apartment because it was right across the street from UN headquarters which might come under attack. So we walked west back to Grand Central. Streams of people were in the streets walking north away from the site of the disaster. When we got to Grand Central, the police had the doors blocked but let us in, a few at a time. Shabbir and I took different trains north, him to Scarsdale and me to Fleetwood, where my sons had their apartments. When I arrived, everyone was there. Benjamin, Mary, Christopher, Jennifer, and me. I said, "Life will never be the same," and I cried. In the next few days, I drafted reflections and statements saying among other things that the US must not respond with violence but address the root causes of poverty and alienation. As we know, the US government did not heed the spirit or letter of my words. Some of what I wrote later appeared in the OSU Journal of Arts and Sciences.

After that catastrophe, air travel in and out of New York was drastically cut back. I was scheduled to fly to South Africa on 13 September, but UNDP canceled the meeting because there was uncertainty about future flights.

A month after 9/11, my lead consultant, Jan Sanders, and I walked around the site of the destroyed Twin Towers in NYC. Jan remembered the following: "We asked ourselves the question, 'How do we shock the world with *human development*?' This was a question that we often asked ourselves when we were both with the ICA. We thought that we could launch a project in Nepal as a partnership between the decentralized governance program and the HIV/AIDS program at UNDP led by Dr. Monica Sharma. This was a way we could help 'shock' Nepal by strengthening local leadership to respond to the growing AIDS epidemic. This response was needed at the time because a civil war was raging in the country which was fueling the spread of the virus. The program was later called Decentralizing Approaches to HIV&AIDS and created local initiatives, committed leaders, and planning processes at the district level to halt the spread of the virus. We met in Nepal to get started; and then I worked with Dr. Tatwa Timsina, founder of ICA Nepal, to implement the program." Thank you, Jan and Tatwa.

I continued to strengthen UNDP by facilitating the team on decentralized governance. I also supported the Urban Management Program (UMP) by chairing another global donor Program Review Committee meetings of the UMP held in New Delhi, India, chairing a meeting of the UMP regional coordinators and the UNDP regional bureaus, helping strategize for UMP Phase IV, and making the UNDP presentation at the UMP Phase IV launch during the global Habitat conference.

In November, Benjamin and Mary flew to South Korea and

had a wonderful time visiting many old friends. Benjamin had told his mother, who was between chemotherapy treatments, "If you don't go now, mom, when will you go?" I was so happy this happened.

I flew to Pretoria, South Africa, where I made a presentation to twenty-five UNDP Resident Representatives on HIV/AIDS-decentralization linkages at a global meeting on HIV-AIDS. The three technical notes I wrote on the topic were later published by UNDP. This was the first time that I was learning in detail and depth about the HIV/AIDS epidemic and the campaign to fight it.

In New York, I helped design the decentralized governance community of practice pilot with McKenzie, lectured at NYU Wagner graduate school of public service, and helped prepare a new website. I finalized in-depth thematic assessments for Nepal and Malawi, case studies on fractured communities, a decentralized governance conceptual framework and methodology, and a conceptual framework on the "role of culture in decentralized governance." I also conducted an innovative seminar on this topic with Dr. Jean Houston presenting, launched a research and design project with grad students from NYU Wagner's International Capstone on the same topic, and prepared a draft policy note on decentralization.

In early December, I was in New Delhi, India, to chair a UMP donor review meeting. My intentions included focusing on poverty reduction, and deepening the lives of the participants. Afterward, I visited a nearby slum project, and then traveled by bus for twelve hours overnight to Dharamsala to visit the home of His Holiness the XIV Dalai Lama. My guide was Yeshi Tenzin. We visited the Tibetan Children's village, Norbulingka Institute, Performing Arts Institute, Namgyal Monastery, a nunnery, the main temple, the residence of His Holiness (he was away at the time), the monastery temple of the His Holiness the Karmapa (participating in a puja [ritual] led by the Karmapa), Nechung Monastery, and the offices of the Government in Exile. It was a blessing to make this pilgrimage. We then took another twelve hour bus ride back to New Delhi. I returned to New York to celebrate Christmas and take two weeks of leave.

18

UNDP DECENTRALIZING THE MDGS THROUGH INNOVATIVE LEADERSHIP (DMIL), MARY'S PASSING, FALLING IN LOVE WITH BONNIE, AND RETIRING: New York City; Garrison, NY; and planet Earth

In 2002, I became UNDP global Principal Policy Adviser for Decentralization, Local Governance, Urban/Rural Development (DLGUD). I coordinated UNDP's global Community of Practice on DLGUD, including a global electronic knowledge network of 985 members. It was fascinating and helpful to carry on global dialogue in this manner. I coordinated the global Decentralized Governance Program, the Local Initiative Facility for Urban Environment (LIFE) in nine countries, and the Cross Practice Project on Localizing the MDGs.

In January, I met Myo Myint, a Burmese consultant at UNDP. We discussed our Buddhist practices. When I asked him which path is best, he said it depends on where you want to go. He said that he wanted to go to Nirvana (the extinguishing of suffering). I said that I wanted to be happy and compassionate.

Later that month, Mary and I went to Oklahoma to care for my mom and help her mark the transition to her living alone in a way that she could embrace in happiness and peace. It was a good visit; and she was doing well.

Back in the Hudson Valley, St. Mary's Episcopal Church in the Highlands, in Cold Spring, New York, received a new priest, Father Shane Scott-Hamblen. Mary and I were happy that he was both a trained theologian and musician. We had been attending this church for a while as well as the Episcopal Church in Garrison. Each Sunday, Fr. Shane celebrated high mass with sung liturgy, incense, and lots of processions.

In Belgrade, Yugoslavia, in February, I provided advice to the government on the creation of a national capacity development facility. On the way back to New York, I stopped in Bratislava, Slovakia, and London, for brief UNDP missions. My other missions that year included to Kyrgyzstan, Nepal, the Philippines, Norway, and Morocco.

At the end of March, I left for Kyrgyzstan. There, I helped design a decentralization strategic framework with the government, visited LIFE projects, and prepared for a national workshop. When I arrived in Almaty, Kazakhstan, at 2:30 am, we stepped out of the plane in a light rain. The driver who was to take me to Bishkek in Kyrgyzstan was nowhere to be seen. We walked in the rain with our luggage to the new airport terminal being built, it appeared, in the shape of ox horns, and there was my driver. He spoke no English and I spoke no Krygyz or Russian. We drove off to Bishkek. It was a wonderful week with many meetings including with the Minister of Local Government, the First Deputy Minister of Finance, the State Secretary, three parliamentarians, five community-based organizations in rural villages, and the head of the UNDP country office. From there I flew to Kathmandu, Nepal.

In Nepal, I helped design and initiate a district pilot on HIV/

AIDS with the country office, and Jan Sander, who had flown in for this purpose. After discussions with the UNDP country office in Kathmandu, we left for the Sunsari district in eastern Nepal. This was to be the location of a pilot on decentralizing HIV/AIDS mitigation. We met with district government officials, and local community residents, and began to design the initiative. Some of the elements included empowering women, providing new self-images to men, using participatory planning, providing leadership training in facilitation, and working with multi-stakeholder teams, theater groups, and the media.

When I returned to New York, I immediately began designing a retreat for the Institutional Development Group, our new work unit at UNDP. We held the retreat in May. In my introduction, I said that this retreat was not about papers and power points; it was about people – the people we serve and the people we are and intend to be.

One day in June, Mary called me at work and said that there was growth in her nodules. Dr. Tiersten wanted to see her tomorrow to change her chemo. At the appointment, her doctor said that she expected very good results from a new chemo. It would be every three weeks for one hour and had few side effects.

In late July, I left for Manila by way of Tokyo. In Manila, I provided policy advice to the UNDP country office, participated in the global launch ceremony for the 2002 Human Development Report, and made a presentation in a global conference. On my way back to New York, my plane made a brief stop in Tokyo. I took a bus to Narita City Center and walked to the Shinshoji Temple where the monks were doing a fire ritual.

Shortly after arriving in New York, I celebrated my 58th birthday and took Mary to two doctors' appointments. I realized that my dreams for my life included healing Mary, publishing a book, developing transformation technologies and being financially secure.

Mary's cancer markers had gone up over the past year, from

thirty to 270. We began nightly Reiki and visualization, in addition to meditation, prayer, chemo, and diet.

In September, I conducted a UNDP mission to Oslo, and returned in time to celebrate our 34th wedding anniversary and Mary's 60th birthday. Her birthday was a great celebration attended by many friends and family including her sister Marjorie and her former college roommate, Sharon House.

Mary on her 60th birthday

In December, Jean Houston, Jan Sanders, Joep and Sony van Arendonk, and I traveled to Marrakech, Morocco, to make presentations in the UNDESA Global Forum on Reinventing Government. One of our contributions was a presentation on reconciling local culture and universal values (love as a dimension of policy making) based on a paper written at my request by the van Arendonks. Shortly before going to Morocco, I had a retinal tear in my right eye which was repaired by laser. Fortunately, during this trip there were no related eye problems.

At the beginning of 2003, I wrote my three-year goals: Mary cured of cancer and in good health; my eyes clear; UN contract maintained; family safe and happy; new levels of creativity, service/compassion, happiness, peace, gratitude, and wisdom. I also began journaling on the computer in addition to my tradition of handwritten journals. Here are a few words from January: "I am grateful for my life just as it is. It is a perfect gift, an unconditional, unqualified, undeserved gift. For any frustration, I am grateful, for it reminds me that I care. For any doubt, I am grateful, for it reminds me that I am awake. For any anger I am grateful, for it means that I care deeply. No clinging! Even, no clinging to no clinging!" If I were to publish all of my journals, they would comprise several books.

Mary and I again attended Jean Houston's Mystery School which we had been doing for many years. If I were to write about each of those sessions in this story, it would take another book or two. They were each amazing, profound, energizing, and helpful is so many ways. Here are a few of the ideas that Jean spoke about in that session – We are made out of light. Our lives are unfolding at the speed of light from beyond time and space. Bohm says that matter is frozen light. What is light? It is of the implicit order. We are coded with cosmic knowing. Earth is God's school, a laboratory of light and dark, the skunk works of the galaxy.

On February 15, 2003, I participated in a peace rally in Manhattan. Mary was in the hospital but insisted that I go. When I arrived at Grand Central, the hall was full of people, many holding colorful placards with creative wording. I circumambulated the hall three times holding the intention that the peace rally would be peaceful. We left the building on Lexington and walked north on Third Avenue. There were moments when I gasped with emotion at the group's solidarity against war, against the White House, and for a peaceful solution with Iraq. I was proud to be an American among fellow citizens who were speaking out and taking collective action.

In March in Washington, D.C., I met with the State Department, the World Bank, USAID, NDI, and the Open Society Institute. It was strange to see the White House knowing who the occupant was. I thought to myself – may his mind become clear; may he turn away from violence. I was waking up to the depth and horror of US government atrocities that had taken place and were taking place often with the support of the American people (by and large of European descent.) At the UN later that month, I lit a candle for peace. This was part of a ceremony for UN staff to express ourselves as individuals. A few hundred staff from every part of the planet took part. I was filled with emotion.

One April day in Garrison, I was waiting for the train to take me to Manhattan. I was watching some West Point cadets on the platform. (West Point was directly across the Hudson River.) I was struck by their youthfulness. They were being molded into fighters and killers. The thought came to me – why not have a global academy to train young warriors of peace and justice. Their training would be as rigorous as the military.

My overview of decentralization worldwide was published by UNDP Philippines as a chapter in the book *Decentralization and Power Shift*. And, I made a presentation in a global workshop in Oslo, Norway. I was reminded that my Work ancestors lived in the Orkney Islands, south of Norway and north of Scotland.

I returned to Stillwater, Oklahoma, with son Benjamin to receive the OSU Outstanding Alumnus Award. Sadly, Mary could not travel because of her cancer treatments. It was meaningful to be back on my undergraduate college campus surrounded by the prairie. I spoke to students in the College of Arts and Sciences and encouraged them to pursue careers of creative, public service. My opening statement was that this is a moment of crisis, of danger and opportunity. In a student forum, I asked them to articulate their twenty-year vision, challenges, and actions. I met Betty Gunter Vogler, my cousin, and her husband, Gary, who had come to the award ceremony. Benjamin said that he might like to do graduate studies there. It would be fourteen years before I would be back at my alma mater.

The Garrison Institute was founded that year by Jonathan and Diana Rose in our village of Garrison. Mary and I were excited that this retreat center was being established just five minutes from our home. I was present when the large Buddha statute arrived from Nepal and I sat on one of the early committees. Over the years, I was fortunate to attend several retreats there with Gelek Rimpoche, a wonderful Tibetan teacher. His Holiness the XIV Dalai Lama came to bless the institute. Soon after, I attended the official opening with original music by Philip Glass.

In late June, I made a trip to Ukraine to provide advice on the formation of a national program on local governance and development. It was very difficult to leave Mary in the midst of her cancer treatments. She assured me that she would be well cared for by our two sons and her doctors and that I should go. Flying over the Atlantic, however, was emotional and teary for me, as I was deeply worried about her. In Ukraine, I worked with the UNDP Ukraine office and traveled around the country including to Chernobyl. One day I received an email from Christopher saying that his mother was not doing well. I felt horrible and decided to return to the US immediately. I called Mary. She said, "I will take care of things here. You take care of things there." Nevertheless, I returned home full of sadness and concern. How was I going to save her?

In July, Mary was having more difficulties with her cancer treatment. The different drugs were causing her pain, confusion, weakness, and nausea. I developed a holistic healing plan in the dimensions of physical, emotional, spiritual, psychological, imaginal, and relational. Mary continued to weaken. I was getting very worried. I called her sister Marjorie in Whidbey Island, telling her what was happening. Marjorie and her husband, John, decided to fly out to be with Mary. I was so grateful that they came. Mary's niece Rebecca also flew out from Arizona to be with

Mary. Benjamin, Christopher, and Jennifer were all wonderful. One day when Benjamin came to our house, he told his mother with tears flowing down his face, "But you are the smartest one in the family." Mary told me that she wanted to renew our wedding vows, so our local Episcopal priest, Father Shane Scott-Hamblen, came to our house and conducted the marriage ceremony in our bedroom with family members around us. We spoke our vows of love and faithfulness till death do us part. I still felt that we must have a breakthrough and save Mary.

One day when we were at the dining table, Mary called out from the bedroom, asking her sister to come to her. When Marjorie returned, she said that Mary told her that she could no longer continue and had to let go. In my heart I was screaming, "No, we must save you." I think that is why she told her sister first. But I knew that the end was near. Dr. Cynthia Ligenza came to administer morphine to make Mary more comfortable. At one point, Mary said that it seemed absurd to be lying there dying.

On July 18 at 3:40 pm, Mary took her last breath and let go. Christopher, Marjorie, John, Rebecca and I were around her. We did rituals and helped her on her way. She looked so radiant and beautiful. Her last breath was utterly calm and peaceful. Rebecca opened a window so her spirit could fly free, a Navajo tradition. We put the icon of the Virgin Mary at her head. Benjamin came to see her body. We put her Indian blanket on her. Her room was full of flowers and plants. I bowed in the four directions and twice to her and chanted "as above, as below." I kissed her feet. Christopher sat holding her hand for a long time. I took off her wedding band. She was now united with the Final Mystery. She had returned to the angelic realm for more assignments. John rubbed her shoulder. Mary was in her fullness. She was love and light. My heart broke into a thousand pieces. My life partner, my love of 35 years was gone. How can life be like this? Mary's face was so peaceful. Her body was taken away to the funeral home.

The next day was a day of shock. The following day, close

friends and family members did a few of Mary's favorite activities at a nearby lake and monastery. Overnight before the Requiem Mass, her body was lying-in-state in the church and Evensong was sung. The memorial service was beautiful. So many friends and family were there at St. Mary's. Father Shane gave a heartfelt homily. I read her obituary. At the end of the service, I burst into sobs. Jan Sanders, my colleague who had come from Canada for the service, came over to comfort me. We then processed out of the church into the light of day. Where was my Mary?

A few days after this, I flew to Ashland, Oregon, to teach in Jean Houston's social artistry school, knowing Mary would want me to do this. When I arrived, I realized that I couldn't do it in my state of grief. I flew back to New York.

As impossible as it seemed, I eventually got up and returned to work in New York City. It was 6 August. I wrote in my journal that day: "May I be kind, generous, and loving to every being I encounter this day. Death is not a failure. Death is the crowning moment of this life. At that crossing, we enter Endless Mystery either in a state of trust and love or fear and anger." The year had accomplishments, but I'm not sure how present I really was to any of them given my ongoing grief. How could I go on without her? At home, I wrote letters on the computer to Mary. And she would write back. Her letters were so kind and encouraging, asking me to go on with living. Of course, I knew that actually I was writing her letters to myself. They were from my mind and heart, which knew so deeply her heart and mind.

By September, my numbness was changing to raw pain, deprivation, lostness, stuckness, absence of interior dialogue, absence of intimacy. I realized that I must change my energy flow, and my perspective. When I had received Mary's ashes, I created a shrine room in my house and in it placed her ashes, her framed photograph, a statue of Kwan Yin, and a meditation cushion. There, I frequently chanted and meditated.

In early November, Jean Houston, Jan Sanders, and I traveled to Mexico City. I had invited them to join me at the UNDESA Global Forum on Reinventing Government in Mexico City. As always, Jean gave a brilliant, provocative talk. As she was leaving the hotel, she fell and broke her ankle. Jan Sanders and I took good care of her; and then Jan helped Jean return home safely. I led a capacity development workshop on decentralized governance at the forum, but turned it over to Paul Lundberg, one of my consultants, in order to help take care of Jean. When I returned to New York, I facilitated the staff retreat for our policy bureau at headquarters.

At home, Christopher spoke about his mother's boundless energy, how she was a nonstop whirlwind of movement – physical, emotional, mental, and spiritual vibration. Now our house was so still and quiet. How do we fill it up again with our energy? She would want that. It was wonderful having Mother with us in Garrison for Christmas.

On January 20, 2004, we celebrated Benjamin's birthday as always. I wrote in my journal: Benjamin, the passionate one, the powerful one, the solitary one, the happy one, the reflective one. May he realize his full potential in this lifetime.

Also in January, I wrote in my journal that sometimes my UN work felt dry, and unmotivating. How could I be "juiced" by life to live with passion and compassion? How could I help liberate all sentient beings?

In February, I facilitated a retreat at headquarters on staff results management.

In March, I wrote in my journal: Use the symbol of being a silver-haired, white, American male to undermine the dominance of silver-haired, white, American men. How? – by being in but not of, respectful yet radical, a dancing bureaucrat, and by being the secular-religious. Also that month, I attended a mindfulness retreat near Oklahoma City led by Larry and Peggy Rowe Ward. That is when I gratefully received my Buddhist name "Ancient Treasure of the Heart." While in Oklahoma, I visited my dear mother. Later that month, I attended a board retreat in Oregon of the International Institute of Social Artistry.

Under my leadership in 2004, the UNDP Practice Note on *Decentralized Governance and Development* was prepared, approved, and translated into five languages. I continued to develop and test a curriculum on "Decentralizing the MDGs through Innovative Leadership." Under my leadership, the DLGUD electronic network expanded and was strengthened with excellent digests and management of queries. The network conducted a lively e-discussion on integrating human rights in decentralized governance, and a DLGUD workspace was developed.

I sent pieces of Mary's jewelry to close friends and family, along with a card, and later, a copy of her provocative poetry and intriguing drawings that I had professionally printed.

I commissioned two concept papers on new approaches in decentralized governance, involving a whole system design approach and a complexity/chaos theory approach. I oversaw the preparation of a concept paper and a knowledge pilot on human rights and decentralization in Bolivia in partnership with the Human Rights Strengthening Program (HURIST), UNDP's Bolivian office and the Swedish International Development Agency (Sida). Under my leadership, an analysis and synthesis of 20 National Human Development Reports on decentralization was carried out in partnership with the Human Development Report Office. Lessons on participatory local governance from the last seven years of the LIFE program were documented and analyzed and were ready to be published as a book.

Back in Garrison, Christopher and Jennifer left on a trip westward to see where they might like to live. Their favorite places were Seattle, Washington, and Asheville, North Carolina. Later that year, they moved to Myrtle Beach, South Carolina, to be near Jennifer's parents. I was grateful that they had stayed with me for one year following Mary's passing. This was an important gift Jennifer and Christopher gave me. Jennifer taught me to cook a bit. Christopher tutored me in preparing the tax return that Mary had always done. It may have been helpful to them as well to have been there. Sometime later, they did move to Asheville.

In that year following Mary's passing, I struggled daily with profound grief and questioned repeatedly the meaning of my life and work. Mary had often told me that my UN work was my hardest spiritual practice. Now showing up and doing the work was intensified in her absence requiring even greater spiritual effort. I also spent much time looking for an apartment in New York City, which I so loved, but could never convince myself to leave my house in Garrison.

Back in New York City, I provided policy support to UNDP's offices in Kosovo, Romania, Albania, China, Cambodia, Bhutan, Thailand, Yemen, Saudi Arabia, Djibouti, Ecuador, Guatemala, Barbados and Kenya.

Over the previous three years, I had commissioned 11 technical papers on innovative cultural and systems perspectives for decentralized governance policy. I felt that they would be helpful in guiding future policy formulation. The innovative papers were written by Dr. Jean Houston, Drs. Joseph and Sony van Arendonk, Dr. Rick Muller, Dr. Harold Nelson, Paul Lundberg, Dr. Tatwa Timsina, Jan Sanders, Jose Elias Graffe, Drs. Larry and Peggy Rowe Ward, an NYU Wagner team of grad students, and myself.

My favorite UNDP program after LIFE was a global initiative on Decentralizing the Millennium Development Goals (MDGs) through Innovative Leadership (DMIL) with activities in Albania, Saint Lucia, Barbados, Kenya and the Philippines. The eight UN MDGs were: 1) to eradicate extreme poverty and hunger; 2) to achieve universal primary education; 3) to promote gender equality and empower women; 4) to reduce child mortality; 5) to improve maternal health; 6) to combat HIV/AIDS, malaria, and other diseases; 7) to ensure environmental sustainability; and 8) to develop a global partnership for development.

I designed this program to make use of and demonstrate three sets of innovative leadership methods—social artistry processes developed by Dr. Jean Houston, the Technology of Participation (ToP) developed by the ICA, and an integral framework developed by Ken Wilber. I called this approach "innovative leadership." The objective was to help countries implement the MDGs at subnational and local levels, utilizing these methods. For this program, I asked Jean Houston to be my senior consultant, along with her colleagues from the International Institute of Social Artistry (IISA), Peggy Rubin and Jan Sanders. This initiative was a partnership with UNDP offices in several countries, regional bureaus, regional centers, the learning resource center, and the IISA.

We designed and conducted workshops in the above five countries that propelled new efforts at localizing the MDGs. In February 2004, we conducted our first event - a seven-day workshop in Albania for 90 leaders with a $5 million follow-up proposal and workshops in the rural areas. In Albania, with its communist history, participants found these methods profound and enlivening. They discovered that one of their traditional cultural stories of the "Princess and the Seven Brothers" could be interpreted as seven ways of implementing the MDGs. We conducted workshops for 50 participants in Barbados and Saint Lucia with a follow-up proposal for an $11 million program at the community level. The Barbados participants saw that cricket, one of their favorite sports, could give them new insights into how to implement the MDGs at local levels. From the UNDESA report "Toward Participatory and Transparent Governance," pages 76-78: "Thus, 1) Caribbean cricket history could be used to identify local targets and indicators which then would bring about; 2) visioning exercises for communities to remember the future by examining the glorious cricket past; 3) concurrently enhancing the awareness of MDGs among the youth by linking this awareness with the cricket history heroes of past, present, and future; and 4) achieving excellence in cricket is linked to achievement of MDGs, thereby granting the localization beyond a single event." My colleague Dr. Rosina Wiltshire was head of UNDP in that country.

We conducted two DMIL workshops for 150 participants in East Africa (Kenya, Uganda, and Tanzania.) Results in Kenya included influencing the MDG Action Plan of the Kenyan government and empowering the Constitutional Reform process of devolution of power from the capital to the provinces. In Kenya, government and nongovernment officials reinterpreted several traditional tribal proverbs as ways of identifying and promoting the MDGs in the villages. In the Philippines, we conducted a three-phase DMIL initiative, including establishing a national core group, holding four workshops in Manila, Tagaytay, and Butuan for 300 participants, and launching 10 follow-up projects to localize the MDGs. The Filipino participants saw that their ancient trading ship was a symbol of their global connections. With the help of Jan Sanders, I prepared a capacity development toolkit, or "integral palette," for decentralized governance. Methods and tools related to DMIL would inspire me in new ways a few years later when I retired from UNDP.

I set up a workshop in Egypt as the pilot country in the Arab states to initiate a program in DMIL in partnership with the Removing Unfreedoms initiative of Amartya Sen and the LIFE Program. I prepared projects in the Philippines and Timor-Leste on decentralizing the MDGs through innovative leadership. I conducted a Trainer of Trainers event in decentralizing the MDGs through innovative leadership for 45 participants, including colleagues from India, Nepal, Albania, Venezuela and Barbados. Under my leadership, the field book on Innovative Leadership and the MDGs we had prepared was tested in seven countries. I also gave a lecture at the UN to students of a master's degree course on Social Artistry Leadership at the invitation of Dr. Houston.

I continued coordinating the global Decentralized Governance Program, resulting in several new knowledge products and the global LIFE program in nine countries with impact in the low-income urban settlements and at the policy level. I coordinated the global trust fund for the Communities of Democracy to prepare for the next global conference in Santiago, Chile.

Teaching in the Social Artistry Leadership Training of Trainers event in Ashland, Oregon, was another highlight of the year. I taught again with Jean Houston, choreographed and danced my first dance in public with Linda Watson, told my first practiced joke in a presentation, sang my first song in public, dramatized a 30-year timeline of DMIL, led a daily meditation group for the first time, participated in a reenactment of Gandhi's salt march, and after the program, went on my first whitewater rafting trip. And I didn't drown!

Under my leadership, the partnership with UNDESA was further strengthened as the Decentralized Governance Group prepared a workshop for the Global Forum on Reinventing Government to be held in Seoul, Republic of Korea. The initiative received USD 900,000 from Sida and the Netherlands and USD 201,000 from Germany's BMZ. I once more presented UNDP's findings on decentralization and poverty reduction at an OECD/DAC workshop in Paris with 70 participants, thus strengthening UNDP's partnership with that organization. I met with the Aga Khan Foundation for substantive discussions on decentralization.

On November 1, my dear aunt Laura Louise, my mother's older sister, passed away in Shawnee, Oklahoma. She was such an elegant, kind person. That month, I came across some of Mary's writings. I realized that she had experienced more pain than I had known about because she kept her own conscience about it. I regretted times of my self-centeredness, or lack of support for her greatness. I vowed to treat other beings with affirmation and kindness.

I helped facilitate the Decentralized Governance Group global retreat in Manila. I was the governance mentor for the Virtual Development Academy. I prepared five cultural practices and a governance case study for a global course in Bangkok. I chaired the task force that prepared the Global Cooperation Framework III cross-practice program on Local Development and Localizing the MDGs. I also presented UNDP's governance approach to 20 DRRs in their training course. And I prepared the UNDP response to the US government concerning the establishment of a UN Democracy Fund.

In January 2005, after I recovered from a bout of pneumonia, John and Thea Patterson, and their daughter, Miriam, ICA colleagues from Canada, visited me holding many wonderful conversations. My early morning sitting meditation was now complemented with playing my French horn and dancing, great ways to prepare to serve the world through the UN. I realized again that my future was to be found in relieving my and all beings' suffering. I was so grateful for having a precious human life. I continued my daily wrestling with when to retire from the UN, where I should live, and what my soul was longing to do and be.

That year, Dr. Pratibha Mehta and I prepared a second book on the LIFE Program based on extensive evaluation, *Pro-Poor Urban Governance: Lessons from LIFE 1992 – 2005.* I was the LIFE global coordinator from 1992 to 1997, and from 2005 to 2006. Pratibha had been the LIFE global coordinator from 1998 to 2004. The book states in the summary on page xii that:

"Through programs in 12 countries and with partnership projects in many more, LIFE had drawn upon a global learning laboratory of over 40 countries to test partnership approaches, community based innovations, and participatory local governance. This was done in a variety of contexts to facilitate the process of scaling up solutions to the tremendous environmental challenges faced by the urban poor. LIFE catalyzed significant resource mobilization. With a budgetary allocation of US$1.7 million in 2001 - 2004 alone, for example, eight LIFE countries mobilized over US$6.8 million of resources in cash and in kind from diverse sources, including national and local government, and local communities themselves. LIFE had also contributed to the growing acknowledgement of participatory local governance as a key mechanism for sustainable development.

"With a small pool of funds and staff and along with many partners from all sectors at the local, national, regional, and global levels, LIFE has had a significant impact at both downstream and upstream levels. It directly benefited the urban poor living in slums and informal settlements by improving living conditions; improving access and infrastructure for water, sanitation, and waste management; reducing air and water pollution; increasing knowledge and awareness about environmental health and practices; increasing access to income generation opportunities; and increasingly addressing issues of land tenure and resettlement. These results have had indirect consequences which have also benefitted the urban poor, such as creating the conditions for improved health, incomes, and income earning capacity."

This was certainly one of my favorite UNDP programs and allowed me to continue the type of work in low-income local communities that I had done during my years with the Institute of Cultural Affairs (ICA).

The success of the LIFE program was due to the work of the national coordinators, national steering committees, bilateral donors, and most of all, the local actors in the local communities, nonprofits, and local government. I was especially grateful to work with a global team of committed, creative national LIFE coordinators.

In March, for the first time, I visited Asheville, North Carolina, to scope it out and spend time with family and friends. Our conversations were very rich, and Larry and Peggy's teachings, profound, including Thich Nhat Hanh's method of stopping, calming, resting, healing, and transforming. I considered moving there to be part of Larry and Peggy's Buddhist community, but, although attracted, decided to stay in New York. Since Mary passed, several friends had given me special care including Bruce Williams, Jan Sanders, Jean Houston, Angel Gail, Linda Bark,

Shabbir Cheema, Thord Palmlund, and others. Jean Houston had been so generous sharing her insights, including that I would help orchestrate a network of networks.

I provided inputs for the UNDP paper on leadership in partnership with the Capacity Development Group and discussions with the Learning Resource Center regarding UNDP's leadership development strategy. I brought two NGO colleagues from Nepal and Ghana to the Community Commons meeting in New York to provide input into the Summary document for the world summit.

In April, Dick Alton asked me again to be the executive director of ICA USA. I thanked him but had to decline. During this year, I had been telecommuting one day per week. In my deep mind, it was becoming clear that I wanted to shift from administrative work to intellectual, artistic, and spiritual work with direct impact on individual and social transformation through facilitation, training, projects, and policies. I realized that the real question was: what else do I need to accomplish in this life?

I sent policy advice to Algeria, Cambodia, and assisted preparations for the Arab Local Governance forum.

In May, Christopher and Jennifer had their wedding shower. After that wonderful event, I spent ten days in Seoul, Korea, at the UNDESA's Sixth Global Forum on Reinventing Government. In that conference, in partnership with UNICEF and CIVICUS, my team and I conducted a workshop on the Role of Civil Society Organizations in Localizing the MDGs. One hundred participants from around the world participated in our workshop, including two UNDP assistant secretaries general. UNDP colleagues from Albania and Barbados shared their experiences on the helpful role of social artistry in localizing the MDGs. I also spoke in the final plenary of the forum. Afterward, I was able to see our dear friends, the Kangs, Parks and Kims. Later, I prepared two short films of our workshop event.

Back in the Hudson Valley on July 1, Christopher and Jennifer were married at St. Mary's Episcopal Church in the Highlands in Cold Spring. (Mary's Requiem Mass had been held there just two years before, after which we dedicated Victorian lampposts outside the church in her memory.) Our baby boy was now married, and to such a wonderful person! It was a beautiful ceremony officiated by Father Shane, followed by a fun reception with great dancing. Mother had come from Oklahoma. Tina and Raymond Spencer, Donrad and Kristin Duncan, and many other guests attended. Christopher and Jennifer were always supportive of each other and now were officially a new family. Blessings on them. What would the future bring? Grandchildren?

After the wedding, I flew to the Philippines to conduct several DMIL workshops with Jean Houston, Jan Sanders and Lowie Rosales. The events were very animated and impactful. I then traveled to Tokyo on my way to Seattle and Ashland to teach in the Social Artistry Intensive. In Narita City near the airport, I stayed overnight in a ryokan on tatami mats, bedding on the floor, sliding paper doors, and a small porch overlooking a garden of rocks, pond, running water, goldfish, and a light. I had eel for dinner, visited the Temple to the God of Fire, sent some emails, and went to sleep. The Social Artistry Intensive was very powerful. UNDP had sponsored several participants from different countries.

Back in April, I had learned that Bonnie Myotai Treace, the abbess of the New York City Zen Center, former vice abbess of Zen Mountain Monastery in the Catskills, had left her order and moved to Garrison. I was amazed. Why had this teacher appeared in my village? Now, in August, I decided to participate in her retreat at the Garrison Institute, just down the road from my house. I dedicated the "sit" (retreat) to relieve my suffering and that of my family, UNDP, America, and all sentient beings everywhere. I drove to the majestic, former Catholic, stone monastery overlooking the Hudson. After the retreat began, and when all of us participants were seated on rows of cushions on the floor of the great hall, two bells rang, and there was activity in the periphery of my lowered gaze. When the teacher passed my cushion, I saw her bare feet sweep by. After bowing to the Buddha and when she was seated, she spoke to us—such clarity, humility, and kindness. When it was my turn to go into Dokusan, a one-to-one meeting of teacher and student, I walked into the small room, bowed, and sat. We had a brief exchange, and I returned to my seat.

Bonnie Myotai Treace Sensei teaching

Back at UNDP, I expanded the online community of practice, DLGUD Net, with regular digests, queries, summaries, and moderated discussions (including on fiscal decentralization). I prepared and led a global retreat for UNDP local governance advisers held in Maputo, Mozambique, resulting in plans for 2006. I prepared a global Junior Professional Officer (JPO) course to be held in Dakar, Senegal, on Decentralized Governance and Development in partnership with the JPO Coordinating Centre,

UN Capital Development Fund and DLGUD advisers. I prepared a website on Decentralizing the MDGs through Innovative Leadership (DMIL) and a video for a Learning Resource Center online course on DMIL.

In October, I happily attended Gelek Rimpoche's profound Four Mindfulness retreat at the Garrison Institute, and soon after, the insight-provoking Landmark Forum in Manhattan. My declaration that arose out of the forum was to live the possibility of courage, and compassion, and create a world that works for everyone. Every day, I struggled to answer three questions – Should I retire early from UNDP? Should I move to Manhattan? What should I do next that fulfills my reason-for-being on this Earth?

I continued coordinating LIFE, including preparation of a strategic options paper, a Bridge Year report, a LIFE book, and a LIFE Net proposal, and managed relations with Sida and the Netherlands. I held a final global LIFE Retreat at Stony Point, New York, with a deeply meaningful, grateful celebration of the past 13 years, calling the program out of being and launching a new LIFE Global-Local Action Network with support of Sida. I held an official launch of the LIFE book at headquarters and distributed copies of the book to all 193 country offices and HQ.

Back on the Hudson, I wondered how the Zen teacher Bonnie Myotai Treace was doing. I saw her one day at the grocery store. We decided to have lunch together in Cold Spring. In that meal at Cathryn's restaurant, I confessed to her that as I approached leaving the UN in the not-too-distant future, it felt like I was facing an abyss. She said, "We can trust the unknown." I said, "Yes, we can trust the Mystery." I learned later that her mother had cancer and that Bonnie was going to Florida to take care of her in her decline. I was still wondering if Bonnie was to be my teacher or friend.

Back at work in Manhattan, I strengthened partnerships with Sida, the Netherlands and BMZ in LIFE and DGP. Sida assigned a program officer and a consultant to help launch the

LIFE Global-Local Action Network. I visited Stockholm, Sweden, and met with two departments of Sida for resource mobilization with follow-up proposals. I developed two resource mobilization proposals, one for LIFE Net and another for DMIL. I strengthened the partnership with the UN Capital Development Fund (UNCDF) with regular meetings and cooperation, and with the International Institute for Social Artistry (IISA), Institute of Cultural Affairs International (ICAI), the Integral Institute, and the Centre for Art and Spirituality in Development (CASID) in the capacity development modules on localizing the MDGs. And I developed a partnership with the Removing Unfreedoms Group (Amartya Sen/Jane Samuels).

In early December, I journeyed to Maputo, Mozambique (on the southeast coast of Africa), to help facilitate the Democratic Governance Group annual retreat. I was able to nurture staff relationships, explore openings for DMIL and LIFE Net, prepare the 2006 DLGUD workplan, and use Wilber and Houston in gender dialogue. That month, I also met with Sida in Stockholm, held the final LIFE retreat in New York, launched the second LIFE book, and prepared a DMIL video.

On New Year's Day 2006, at Sunday morning Mass at St. Mary's in Cold Spring, French horns heralded the new year. I had invited Bonnie to church, but she had said "Why don't you come by my cabin for soup and freshly baked bread." I went. We talked. I left. When I returned home, I was shaking. I was vibrating. "Who is she?" I asked myself. "What am I feeling? Why am I so moved?" I realized then that she probably would not be my teacher. Was I falling in love with her?

A few days later, I did something that surprised myself. I sent Bonnie a dozen yellow roses. She would tell me later that she didn't quite know what to make of this, and even mentioned it to her mother as something confusing. Her mother, who I would come to see had a lovely sense of humor, said "oh, I think it's pretty darn obvious; he is smitten with you." Bonnie wondered though if I were someone who just sent flowers to Buddhist teachers. Over tea the next day, we did a little dance of sorts: she said, "Rob, you know your spiritual life is the most important thing to me." I nodded, yes, not understanding. "Well, what this means is that if you want to do my retreats, that is great. But if you want to go out to dinner with me, then you can't do my retreats. So, you just need to let me know." I was suddenly crystal clear. "I want to go out to dinner," I smiled. (Later my mother would laugh, "I like her; she made you choose.")

Around the time we were beginning to see one another, Bonnie had gotten the devastating news that her mother had terminal cancer. Her mother asked if Bonnie would be "her one," the one who would walk the final mile along with her. Bonnie put a hold on all her work leading her Zen community, put everything she owned into storage and moved to Florida, putting herself completely into being her mother's caretaker. She would come back to New York to lead a retreat, giving talks and seeing her students, every other month, and then return to 24-7 caregiving. I could barely imagine what it was like for her. One time when she flew back to New York, I hired a taxi, bought some flowers, and met her at the airport. We rode back together full of feelings. When we got back to Garrison, we both knew that we loved each other. Thereafter, we took many walks together. We talked and talked some more. She visited my house and met Boots, my black cat with white boots, and saw the room with Mary's ashes and the statue of Kwan Yin, the bodhisattva (a person dedicated to relieving the suffering of all beings) of compassion.

Bonnie's mother was weakening, had developed dementia, and Bonnie was exhausted, though honored to be caring for her. In what turned out to be her mother's final two months, Bonnie had to arrange for assisted living care. The best place was too far for Bonnie to commute, so she rented a small cottage several blocks from the home so she could be there every day. It was on the gulf in Mexico Beach, near Panama City. We would often talk by phone at the end of her long days, and I would fly down several times to visit her there. Bonnie loved the water, and it was hugely healing for her. Then in April her mother passed. Her mother had asked Bonnie to lead the memorial service; which she did beautifully, though I knew it was excruciating for her. She stayed another month and then returned "home" to New York.

In late January, I gained new insights on leadership in a "presencing" workshop led by MIT's Otto Scharmer at the Garrison Institute. His "U" theory of letting go and inventing the new was very helpful.

In five months, it would be July 31, the day I would turn 62, the official retirement age in the UN. I began preparing for my succession. On the one hand, it seemed odd to retire at such an early age when I was beginning to understand the UN and my role in it. On the other hand, I realized that it was good to bring young people into the organization. I knew that I would miss being part of the UN, but I looked forward to new challenges and adventures of serving and living. And yet, I was uncertain what the future would bring.

Bonnie and I began to talk of marriage. I felt as if I were 18. I was so much in love. We exchanged poems. We were both surprised that this was happening. Bonnie had come back to New York needing to rebuild her organization, recreate relationships with her students, do fundraising…and find a new place to live. And yet in the midst of all this, we were blossoming. It was as if we met in the deepest of places right at the beginning: grief, commitment to relieving suffering, the mystery of it all.

Senior management asked me to write a book of my reflections and analysis of my experience and lessons of the past 16 years with UNDP. It was challenging to pull together so much knowledge in this time frame. I went over everything I had published, all of the project reports and evaluations, all of my performance reviews, all of my speeches, all of my country and donor mission reports, and more, and reflected deeply on my lessons and recommendations.

On July 13, I presented my manuscript to senior management at UNDP for a book entitled *Power and Prosperity to the People: Decentralizing Governance for Human Development*. It was in three sections. The first section with three chapters was on a conceptual framework of decentralized governance for human development. Next came the longest section on experiences and learnings. This included chapters of lessons on decentralization and local governance; how to improve the urban slums through local initiatives (LIFE); how to decentralize the MDGs through innovative leadership (DMIL) capacity development; and how to create a global community of practice on decentralization, local governance, urban/rural development (DLGUD). The final section was on looking to the future and included chapters on cultural and systemic policy perspectives on decentralizing governance; reflections on international development; and conclusions and recommendations.

It was hard to leave a place and global network full of many close colleagues whom I respected and with whom I liked working, a place with a mission that I believed in, an organization that enabled me to serve local people around our planet, a vehicle that enabled me to project my own sense of mission and that had provided me with a multitude of valuable experiences and lessons in being an international civil servant and a compassionate human being.

One fine day, my kind son Benjamin helped me pack and move my books, files, and memorabilia from my UNDP office in Manhattan to my home office in Garrison. Gratitude to Benjamin.

I was overflowing with gratitude. I was ready for the next adventure of loving people and planet.

On July 29, my family and I held a grand event at Hillside Cottage, my home, in Garrison, celebrating my UN retirement and next life chapter, mother's birthday, Christopher and Jennifer's wedding anniversary, Benjamin's adoption anniversary, and the anniversary of Mary's passing. I called the celebration the "Dance of Life." Sixty family members and friends attended coming from the UN, ICA, Mystery School, Hermitage Heart (Bonnie's nonprofit), the Garrison community, New York City, California, and Canada, Another sixty sent congratulatory messages. We ate and sang, made music and danced, and made speeches. I was so happy to introduce Bonnie to my circles of people, and to meet hers, and to share the miracle of our new love. So many of the people in my life had witnessed my deepest sadness and the challenges of Mary's illness and then passing. It felt wonderful to have this new chapter beginning that I could share with them as well: full of possibility, beauty, loving and celebrating. I could never have guessed that my life would take such an amazing turn, and I felt my friends and family deeply moved as well. Sherry Cheema asked Bonnie and me to sit in two chairs, and while music played, she danced up to us and thanked us for being such examples of faith and starting fresh. We were embarrassed by the attention, but will never forget the moment.

My niece Debra Bachert made a delicious cake for the event. Neighbor Joy Plaisted played her harp. UNDP colleague John Lawrence played the violin. Sister-in-law Lisa Lindberg performed a dance accompanied by my brother Duncan and nephew Matthew. Suzi Tortora, my dance teacher, led the group in a dance. Colleague Jan Sanders was the MC. Friend Linda Bark read a poem. Bonnie's student Katie Hantz played "I Hope You Dance" on her guitar while I danced. The entire group danced the ancient Greek dance Enos Mythos. As the American-English poet T. S. Eliot wrote "There is only the Dance!"

Through these 16 years of my life and my work with UNDP, I introduced, demonstrated, and used innovative planning and leadership methods. These included the ICA's Technology of Participation (ToP) methods of group facilitation, participatory strategic planning, the workshop method, and focused conversations; Jean Houston's social artistry processes; Ken Wilber's integral thinking frameworks; Harrison Owen's

Open Space; Appreciative Inquiry; Lee Hock's chaordic theory; complexity theory; chaos theory; and other methods and models.

My work in concert with the efforts of many others helped improve the lives of millions of people, in thousands of low-income settlements, in hundreds of cities around the world through the development of new policies, programs, and projects of decentralization, local governance, and urban development. I became an international civil servant of people and planet. I took care of my mind, heart, and body so that I would be healthy and could help make others happy.

I learned that doing international development is about inviting people to participate in realizing their own potential as human beings, as cultures, and as societies. I learned that promoting new policies, programs, and projects of decentralizing governance to subnational levels releases tremendous energy and creativity for sustainable human development, and provides a counterpoint of localization to the forces of globalization. I learned that being a human being is about service, compassion, collaboration, risk taking, creativity, model building, using effective methods, taking good care of yourself, and making others happy.

I was schooled in having a vision, creating a plan, being intentional, collaborating with others, giving it my all, letting go, and letting be. This prepared me for once more stepping into the void of unknowing, knowing that all is mystery, all is well, and all will be well. I developed contacts and colleagues around the world with whom I could continue to work.

I loved my parents, parents-in-law, and wife Mary until death parted us. I loved my two sons and daughter-in-law. I loved my new sweetheart, Bonnie, as we journeyed toward marriage. I experienced again that life includes the death of everything and everyone I love, but that love cannot die but will find a way to live forever.

Once again, I was stepping into the void. Can the unknown really be trusted?

PART FOUR

EQUIPPING INNOVATIVE LEADERS FOR SUSTAINABLE DEVELOPMENT, AND CREATING A NEW LIFE

Teaching innovative leadership at New York University (NYU) Wagner Graduate School of Public Service, consulting, giving keynotes, blogging, and book writing: mid 2006 – mid 2017: 62 to 73 in New York, North Carolina, and Planet Earth

In August 2006, Iran defied a UN deadline to halt its nuclear activities or face sanctions, saying that its program was not designed to create weapons.

> *"Hope is not like a lottery ticket you can sit on the sofa and clutch. . . . Hope is an ax you break down doors with in an emergency. . . . Hope should shove you out the door, because it will take everything you have to steer the future away from endless war, from the annihilation of the Earth's treasures and the grinding down of the poor and marginal."*
> -Rebecca Solnit

19

INNOVATIVE LEADERSHIP CONSULTING, MARRYING BONNIE, AND BECOMING GRANDPARENTS:
Garrison, NY; Asheville, NC; and planet Earth

After retiring from UNDP on July 31, 2006, I set out to offer my services of facilitation and training in innovative leadership and community and organizational development utilizing systems thinking, strategic planning, implementation for results, continuous learning, and social artistry. I decided on this focus because of the need for new leadership styles and skills to promote sustainable development.

Of course, it was not easy to let go of 16 years at the UN and a total of 37 years in international development. Who was I now? What was the future to bring? To explore these and other questions, I began a kind of "sabbatical" to allow myself to reflect, study, and reinvent my life and work.

My first consultancy was with UNDP to design a five-year program on localizing the MDGs in slums and squatter settlements in 19 countries. My consulting partner was Dr. Emad Adly, the LIFE and Global Environment Facility (GEF) Small Grants Program coordinator in Egypt. UNDP decided not to go ahead with the new phase of LIFE. We were very disappointed.

I initiated Innovative Leadership Services as my marketing vehicle with a website, email address, and name cards each with a photo of the Earth.

Bonnie and I continued our conversations about marriage. We had very different ways of discerning: I was rational and liked to make lists and have us do processes. This was how we did things in the ICA and the UN, and what I was familiar with from my life with Mary. Bonnie was deeply intuitive and profoundly tender, and could be hurt by my intellectual or analytical approach. We had to learn how to hear one another, and respect each other's way of being and doing. We talked long and deep about who we were and why we would come together. We each had been leaders in religious orders for 20 years, she as abbot of her own temple and a highly regarded Zen teacher. She had been an ordained nun, lived with a shaved head and her vows included not having children. We were each born in the Year of the Monkey. We each were English majors in undergraduate school. Yet, we were very different. I was almost 12 years older. I was an activist with the heart of a monk. And she was a nun with the heart of an activist. She was a Pisces and I a Leo. We recognized the challenges of coming together with our own histories of other relationships and with my two children. In fact, when my wife died after 35 years of marriage, I did not plan to remarry and wanted to be a "hermit monk" after years as a "red knight." She was no longer living in a large monastic community, but content living in the woods alone, with birds and streams her main companions. Yet here we were, drawn to each other.

What would we be for each other and for the world? How could we enable each other's life and work and together celebrate our couplehood? Bonnie was the priest and Zen teacher of Hermitage Heart, a nonprofit organization she founded when she left the

Mountains and Rivers Order after 24 years and being the vice abbess of Zen Mountain Monastery and abbess of the Zen Center of New York City. I was a widower, retiring after 16 years as a UNDP policy adviser and was reinventing my life/work one more time. We were each facing the unknown and wanted to face it together.

In January 2007, I began designing a course to teach at NYU Wagner. I declined kind offers to be the spiritual director at Abbey North, a program coordinator in the High Commission for Legal Empowerment of the Poor, or a local governance policy adviser in Afghanistan.

Three and one half years after Mary's passing, Bonnie and I traveled in February to Phoenix, Arizona, to scatter Mary's ashes on Squaw Peak where her mother and father's ashes had been placed. It was a profound event with many family members and close friends climbing together, ritualizing in a circle, speaking, some tears, and singing as we celebrated and let go once more. I was grateful that Bonnie with her love and priestly perspective was part of this.

That year, I rushed to Edmond to care for my mother after her debilitating pneumonia. It was very serious and was the first time in her life that she was laid low. I stayed over one month. As she struggled to regain her capacities, we realized that a major shift had happened for all of us and that she would need to be in assisted living. Bonnie came to see her, and we returned to New York together. We also went to Asheville to be with family, to Whidbey Island to attend Marjorie's beautiful fabric art exhibition, to Ashland, Oregon, to teach social artistry with Jean Houston, and to Halliburton, Canada, to visit John and Thea Patterson at Abbey North. During my "sabbatical", I wanted to design a book based on my journals, poems, essays, articles, drawings, and photographs, but this was not to happen. Jennifer Read Hawthorne of the Chicken Soup for the Soul series asked me to write a story that was published in *Life Lessons for Loving the Way You Live.*

Bonnie and I decided to get married that year on September 2 in the great hall of the Garrison Institute, where we had first met two summers earlier.

Before our wedding, we traveled to Athens, Greece, where we met up with a group of colleagues to celebrate the seventieth birthday of Jean Houston. The eleven of us took a mythic journey by boat, our own Odyssey, from Athens to Ithaca and back. With Jean's love of myth, and especially this one, this was the perfect choice of a gift from Peggy Rubin to celebrate Jean's mythic life. On the way to Ithaca, I asked, what is it to go home? What is our true home? As we approached the island I asked myself, what is my Ithaca? What does a social pioneer look like in 2007? On the return journey, the group stopped at Delphi. There, Bonnie and I held a mystical union ceremony at the site of the Delphic oracle. After the boat trip, Bonnie and I traveled to Vienna to a UN conference for which I was a consultant. Under contract with UNDESA, I had trained the workshop facilitators for the conference and was then providing support and oversight. When the conference ended, Bonnie and I returned to New York to make final preparations for our wedding.

On September 2, a stunning day, we gathered with friends and family to celebrate our covenant at the Garrison Institute, overlooking the Hudson River. Jean Houston's Mystery School, in which some of our wedding party participated at the Institute, ended at 11 am. In the early afternoon, our wedding ceremony began with the prelude of Bruckner's Fourth Symphony played on French horn and organ; and a water blessing was performed to sanctify the space. The processional commenced with the sounding of the shofar followed by the andante of Tchaikovsky's Fifth Symphony with organ and horn. My sisters-in-law Lisa Lindberg and Marjorie Bachert walked me down the aisle in the great hall, followed by Bonnie accompanied by her brother David and uncle Bill. The three celebrants met us on the dais: Dr. Jean Houston, my Episcopal priest Father Shane Scott-Hamblen, and

Enkyo Roshi, a Buddhist priest from New York City and friend of Bonnie. At the front of the hall was a huge photo of our home planet Earth. Bonnie and I had written our vows reflecting our life understandings.

Katy Hantz sang a beautiful song. Robert Esformes, a cantor, sang a traditional song while we circled each other in the Jewish tradition. Each of the celebrants led a part of the ceremony. Bonnie's best women, Susan Lipsey, Bonnie's sister Lee Ann Nail, Joy Plaisted, and Martha Rome, and my best men, Shabbir Cheema, Duncan Work, and my two sons, Benjamin and Christopher, were seated at our sides. The young daughters of two of Bonnie's students were flower girls. It was a beautiful and deeply meaningful service, after which we processed out of the hall to J. S. Bach's "Jesu, Joy of Man's Desiring" again by horn and organ. Everyone walked outside in front of the monastery overlooking the Hudson for photos and conversation. It was an exquisite day. A delicious meal was next, followed by dancing downstairs. What a day it was of recreating each of our lives. Jennifer, Christopher's wife, was pregnant, so our first grandchild was symbolically present for the event.

Bonnie Myotai and me speaking our wedding vows to each other

For our honeymoon we traveled north to Niagara Falls, and on to John and Thea Patterson's gracious home, retreat center Abbey North, lake and cabin, which they had kindly invited us to enjoy. We continued our several months-long conversation concerning how to have a "fresh start", move out of Hillside Cottage, and have a new place to live that we could create together. It was difficult for Bonnie to live in "my" house; and it was difficult for me to let go of my family home.

In early October at my arrangement, Sarah Miller of ICA International and I met with a senior UNDP official in New York City concerning UNDP sponsorship of a global conference in Tokyo in November 2008. Later in October, Duncan, Lisa, and I helped move mother to assisted living while clearing out her cottage and celebrating many beautiful memories and objects.

In November and December, as part of my consultancy with UNDESA which Shabbir arranged, I wrote a twenty-six page paper, "Strengthening Governance and Public Administration

Capacities for Development," for the UN Economic and Social Council. It contained many leadership methods and models from my work with ICA, UNDP, and Jean Houston, as well as my study of Buddhist philosophy and the integral theory of Ken Wilber. It was presented to the UN's Seventh Session of the Committee of Experts on Public Administration in April 2008 to help guide their deliberations.

In January 2008, I spent a week with mother who was in assisted living. She was having many struggles which we worked to resolve. Also that month, Bonnie and I taught on the faculty of the Social Artistry Trainer of Trainers Program in Ashland, Oregon.

On February 8 in Asheville, North Carolina, our first grandchild was born, Phoenix Orion Work (POW). I was very excited to be a grandfather of this little human and looked forward to helping him grow up as he would help me grow old. What an auspicious name he received from his parents: the mythic phoenix bird rising again and again from its own ashes; and Orion, the hunter, constellation of stars. Soon after his birth, I visited Asheville to meet him—what a joy to hold him.

In March, Jean Houston began teaching weekend sessions of advanced mystery school at the Garrison Institute. Bonnie and I attended these rich feasts of wisdom, creativity and motivation and sometimes spoke to the whole group at Jean's request. Also that month, I began a holistic regimen to heal my thyroid which had developed nodules. Angel Gail and Linda Bark continued providing their intuitive advice by phone. They both advised me not simply to do the right thing and enable others but to follow my heart and write from my deepest source. Angel Gail also said that there was something ageless about me, that I would live a very long time, that I am attracted to powerful women, and that Bonnie and I would become hermit writers together.

When I returned to Asheville, Bonnie was hard at work in Garrison preparing for her first *jukai*, the ceremony in which fifteen of her Hermitage Heart students received their Buddhist names and took their vows. The ceremony went well, but toward the end of the retreat she developed a severe headache unlike anything she had experienced. (Later, it would be surmised this was caused by the bite of a Lyme disease-infested tick.) By the time I returned to Garrison, her head pain was disabling. We began searching for treatments to relieve the pain and understand what had happened.

In April, I was on the faculty of the weeklong Social Artistry School in Ashland, Oregon. Jean asked me to talk about the globe, what Mary had taught me, and how I met Bonnie. I also gave a presentation on my use of social artistry in UNDP, and led a meditation and a dance. I spoke about our time of crisis and how social artistry may provide the healing antidote. When Bonnie was feeling better in New York, she flew out to teach in the school. In her first session, she invited people to take off their masks, see eye to eye, heart to eye, mind to mind, and cultivate the empty field. Later, she led a sitting meditation and gave a Dharma talk on Dogen's "backward step."

In mid-May, I returned to Asheville to be with family and to look at assisted living facilities in Asheville for Mother. When I returned to New York, I continued preparing for my first NYU course in June.

20

TEACHING GRAD SCHOOL AT NYU WAGNER, AND MOTHER'S PASSING: Garrison, NY; Cold Spring, NY; Swannanoa, NC; New York City; planet Earth

In early June 2008, I taught my first course at NYU Wagner Graduate School of Public Service at the Washington Square campus in Manhattan. NYU Wagner was one of the top grad schools of public service in the US and was part of New York University, one of the world's largest and best private universities, with campuses in several countries. I had designed the course based on my final UNDP program, Decentralizing the MDGs through Innovative Leadership (DMIL), and it was titled "Innovative Leadership for Human Development." It was a four-credit-hour, one-week, five-day intensive, five hours per day. NYU Wagner Professor Paul Smoke had asked me to design and teach the course not because I was an academic but because of my 38 years of public service with the UN and a nonprofit. Paul shepherded my various iterations of the syllabus through the academic committees. I had met Paul when I asked MIT to help UNDP with a global research project. Paul was the MIT professor who helped us.

Before the course began, I moved to Manhattan for the week, staying with Mystery School friend Maria Elena Granger in her apartment. I was nervous before teaching the first class. But once we began and I heard the voices and concerns of students, I loved it. The fifteen students were from various countries and were eager to learn effective methods of leadership to promote human development. Before the class started, I put a table at the front of the classroom. Behind the table on the wall, I placed an Earth flag. On this "altar" were a beautiful cloth and provocative art objects. I also had snacks for the students.

The course was designed to explore an integral framework for international development and leadership that complemented the current technocratic, bureaucratic, hyperrational, statistical approach. Integral development, based on the work of Ken Wilber, included: 1) systems/institutions/ policies; 2) cultural development; 3) individual behavior; and 4) individual consciousness and values. The course enabled students to experience and practice innovative leadership methods that could make a dramatic difference in their life and work. As an alternative to a "command and control" leadership style, innovative leadership was facilitative, participatory, collaborative, creative, and profound. Four levels of innovative leadership or social artistry elaborated by Dr. Jean Houston were experienced, enhanced, and practiced: 1) physical/ sensory capacities; 2) psychological/historical capacities; 3) mythic/symbolic capacities; and 4) unitive/intuitive capacities. UN program experience (2002 to 2006) was shared related to the role of innovative leadership in achieving the MDGs in Nepal, Albania, the Eastern Caribbean, Kenya and the Philippines. In addition to readings from several books, the course made use of the Integral Palette of Capacity Development with its 52 methods that Jan Sanders and I collected for UNDP's DMIL program. Students were introduced to and enabled to practice methods of systems design, organizational facilitation, cultural interpretation, and individual awareness.

I began the class with meditation, which I simply called "a time of silence and stillness." After that experience, I asked people to introduce themselves. Next, we held an opening conversation about international development so that they could begin to think about it and I could get a sense of their current understanding. I then gave an opening presentation on the history of international development and our current moment of crisis and opportunity. Following that, we discussed what had happened during class that morning: what did they remember? What was the mood of the group? What did they learn? What would they use in their future work and life? Students then went out for lunch in nearby restaurants.

When they returned, I invited them to do a group circle dance to the music of Pachelbel's Canon to experience themselves as a community. Some loved it, and some were a bit apprehensive. Next, I demonstrated an innovative leadership method of integral thinking in four dimensions of changing mindsets, behaviors, cultures, and systems, after which students practiced the method in small teams. At the end of the class, we reflected on what had happened that afternoon and throughout the entire day. I reminded them of their assignments for the next day, including readings, journal writing, and a brief paper. We were off and running. I had been so nervous and unsure before the class started, yet it seemed to be working. Gratitude.

On the fourth day that week, two guest artists worked with the class after lunch. Aynsley Vanderbrouche, a New York City choreographer and dancer, led the students in a movement exercise. And Joy Plaisted, a Juilliard-trained harpist, led a music exercise. I then facilitated a workshop in which the students created a new story, song, and symbol for New York City. On the final day with the theme of individual awareness, Bonnie introduced and led Zen meditation with the class. The students wrote in their journals how much they appreciated these three experts. From Grand Central,

I returned to Cold Spring on Metro-North, a happy teacher of innovative leadership.

After my teaching, Bonnie and I drove to Asheville to spend the summer near our new grandson and family. This began ten years of traveling between New York and North Carolina, spending fall and spring teaching and consulting in New York and summer and winter writing near family in North Carolina. It was a twelve-hour drive each way, which we broke halfway with an overnight in New Market, Virginia. We did the round trip twice per year. Bonnie was still suffering from the swelling and head pain that had begun that May. We hoped that time in Asheville and medical care there might help. She had to cancel several retreats and was desperate to find her way back to teaching her students. She developed a beautiful ceremony—the 108 Water Bowl Mala—for the Parliament of World Religion in Australia and would perform it and serve many students with it over the several years, including at Thomas Berry's memorial at St. John the Divine, before we finally got the tumor removed that was eventually discovered as the cause of her disability.

My brother, Duncan, and I decided that our mother should move from Edmond, Oklahoma, to Asheville, North Carolina. At first, I wasn't sure that at her age she should go through the trauma of moving. Lisa led the packing, giving away, and selling with help from Duncan and me. After we returned to Asheville, Christopher flew to Edmond on July 1, his wedding anniversary, and brought his grandmother to Asheville. We wanted to be able to take better care of her by having her with us. We researched elders' facilities and found Arden Woods, which we felt was good and not the most expensive.

In mid-August, after extensive research and preparations, Bonnie and I traveled to Rochester, Minnesota, to visit Mayo Clinic for treatment of her head pain. She saw many doctors, took many tests, and left with some recommended medications for pain relief. Each one had many side effects; none of them ultimately helped.

At the end of August, I reflected in my journal that I still had a role to play in making a better world. I had methods. I would write. I would carry on the OE/EI/ICA lineage. I would not be proud. I would honor my colleagues and make my unique contribution. I would keep my own conscience. I would dance, write, inspire others, and use my life to make something happen.

In October, Bonnie and I rented a beautiful log cabin east of Asheville in Swannanoa. Its large fireplace was made of big stones from Davy Crockett's old cabin. We thought this was a legend until we learned that one of Davy Crockett's descendants, an elderly lady, actually lived across the road from us. We loved this cabin and had many family celebrations over several years inside and on the big porch. We named it Hawks' Nest because we had seen one in a tall tree near the cabin. This felt wonderful that Bonnie and I were for the first time creating a new home together.

When we returned to the north, Bonnie and I knocked on doors in Pennsylvania to get out the vote for Obama.

Also that year, a minigrants program was established in Nepal for microprojects in social artistry in collaboration with ICA Nepal and the International Institute of Social Artistry (IISA) and through the newly constituted Robertson Work Fund for Social Artistry. I was touched by this designation.

Because of family responsibilities, I said no to work requests that year in Nepal and Kenya with the Jean Houston Foundation, and in Honolulu with the East-West Center and Shabbir Cheema. I also declined a request to teach the International Capstone course at NYU Wagner starting in January, so that we could stay in Asheville in the winter. It was good that we did.

In January 2009, my precious mother became ill from swallowing food down her windpipe. We took her to Mission Hospital; and on the 24th, she passed away peacefully surrounded by her devoted family. She was eighty-eight years old. What a loving, creative, evolving person she was. I had thought that she would live into her 90s since her mother, Sally, had lived to 95 and her mother's sister Mary Yates Dodd had lived to 103. Duncan and I each have many of her beautiful watercolor paintings in our homes along with many heartfelt memories of her. I was grateful that she got to meet and be with her first great-grandchild, Phoenix, who took his first step the day after mother took her last. We celebrated Mother's completed life with six services: three hours after her death; at Jubilee!; three hours at the crematory; at a Cloud Cottage memorial; at her earlier retirement home in Edmond, Oklahoma, and at a graveside service in Durant, Oklahoma, her hometown, where her ashes were buried in the family plot at Highland Cemetery, near her husband, parents, and grandparents. Some of my words in the Edmond service included: To mother Mary, brown-eyed girl, flashing smile, you lived your life fully, gratefully, joyfully, thank you for your great kindness, thank you for filling our world with beauty, affirmation, and diligence, thank you for being open and becoming ever new because of your deep interest in this world, thank you for loving us, for loving me, thank you for being you – unrepeatable, unforgettable you. I missed her every day.

Mother's watercolor painting of Oklahoma magnolia
blossoms in an antique family soup tureen

In February, I was able to complete a paper for the East-West Center on civil society innovations in governance leadership. It was published later as a chapter in the book *Engaging Civil Society*, edited by Shabbir Cheema and Vesselin Popovski. Shabbir also invited me to conduct a consultancy in a middle-eastern country to strengthen their local governance institutions. Although I wanted to help do this, I finally agreed with Bonnie's recommendation, and declined to go so as not to give my approval to the government's gender policies. This was the first time I did not work in a country because of their policies. I didn't know if I had made the right decision, but it was the one I made.

On May 3, 2009, Bonnie and I moved out of Hillside Cottage in Garrison to an apartment in Cold Spring on the Hudson riverfront. It was heaven seeing the river each day at every hour and in every weather and season. The waterfront, gazebo, and park below were the sites of many town festivities throughout the year, with music wafting up to our apartment. Directly west across the river was Crows' Nest Mountain. We named our home Crows' Nest. A bit north and on the river was the dramatic Storm King Mountain. Several miles south, the river flowed around the island of Manhattan and out into the Atlantic. It also flowed northward as a tidal estuary of the Atlantic: fresh water flowing south; saltwater flowing north. The native peoples had named it *Mahicanituck*, "the river that flows both ways." It had been hard to leave 251 with its many memories; and even though I had always hated moving in any case, this time new life beckoned, and I decided and did it willfully.

Immediately after moving to Cold Spring, I again taught Innovative Leadership for Human Development at NYU Wagner. Dr. Monica Sharma was a guest presenter one afternoon and shared her work on the UN's HIV/AIDS leadership program. Monica was the director of the program and had collaborated with me on the Nepal Decentralizing HIV/AIDS Mitigation program when we were both in UNDP. The highlight of the course for me was always the students. I especially appreciated the ones who had some work experience before doing their graduate studies. Most students had plans for how they would use their Wagner master's degree in their future public service. One student from Ghana planned to run for president of his country. I enjoyed discussing graduate teaching with Dr. Erica Foldy, the coordinator of management courses at Wagner.

My NYU Wagner Innovative Leadership class 2009

I was a global adviser and a conference facilitator for the State of the World Climate Leadership Forum, held in early August in Belo Horizonte, Brazil. That is when I became convinced that we had only ten years before climate chaos would begin to cause great harm. I began to focus more of my attention and energies through my keynotes, consulting, writing, and activism on raising the alarm and promoting climate chaos mitigation and adaptation within a systems view of social transformation. I met many new colleagues on the conference team, including Dr. Richard David

Hames, the futurist; Dr. Nancy Roof, the founder of *Kosmos Journal*; and Dr. Daniel Christian Wahl, promoter of regenerative cultures.

In October, I participated once again in a retreat with Gelek Rimpoche at the Garrison Institute. It was a blessing to receive his teachings on emptiness (interdependence) as the basis of wisdom and compassion.

In November, I had a sleep study and began using a bipap machine to give me more efficient sleep. It helped a lot. At the end of the month, I had a bothersome but successful exploratory intestinal surgery to remove a blockage.

In order to spend the winter in Asheville, I declined an invitation I would have loved to accept from the Earth Institute at Columbia University to help teach a grad course on environmental science policy starting January 2010. And more importantly, earlier, because of the role of fossil fuels in driving climate chaos, I decided not to accept a community development consulting contract in Vietnam related to Chevron's expansion of off shore drilling. As a consultant I continued to weigh up the social and ecological impacts of any consulting work.

21

MAKING KEYNOTES, BEING A FULBRIGHT SPECIALIST, FACILITATING, AND SURGERY: Cold Spring, NY; Swannanoa, NC; New York City; planet Earth

In March 2010, at the invitation of Dr. Terry Bergdall, CEO of ICA USA, I gave the keynote for an international development think tank held in Chicago at the ICA USA headquarters. I had not been there for many years and was excited to be back in Chicago and at the ICA with which I had loved working for 22 years before my UN days. I was nervous about speaking to my colleagues concerning my life and views; and I spoke much longer than my allotted time. There is a video on YouTube of my presentation. This was the first time that I declared in a public talk, outside of my NYU Wagner class lectures, that "ours is the most critical decade and century in human history" because of ecological, social, economic, and political crises. My talk seemed to shock some of the colleagues but overall was well received. I continued in all of my following interventions to speak and write that message along with what we should do to respond to these systemic crises.

In May of 2010 for the third year, I taught a graduate course on innovative leadership for sustainable human development at NYU Wagner. Kathleen Callahan, a Columbia University adjunct professor, shared her experience in systems change in the Environmental Protection Agency when she was a senior official there. I again invited Bonnie to lead a session in the final module on individual awareness. She introduced Zen meditation and led them in a meditation experience. Students again wrote in their journals that they found this very helpful. I also spoke to the NYU Wagner International Public Service Association, challenging students to respond from their hearts to the cries of the world.

My 2010 NYU Wagner students from 14 countries in
Innovative Leadership for Sustainable Development

I traveled from Cold Spring to Asheville to be present for the birth on June 14 of our second grandchild, Mariela Katherine

Work, her names related to her grandmothers, Mary and Kathleen. What a glorious day it was. She was the first female child on the Work side in four generations. I sensed immediately that she might become a self-confident leader of the people. There was an amazing focus and determination in her gaze, especially for such a small child. It was pure joy to be with her.

In late June, at the invitation of my former UNDP colleague Shabbir Cheema, who had become director of governance programs at the East-West Center (EWC) in Honolulu, I designed and facilitated an international workshop in Honolulu on sustainable policymaking for sustainable development. The experts identified current factors, articulated a future vision, and created strategies and actions. Happily, I was able to buy her ticket, and Bonnie was able to go with me to Honolulu. Bonnie decided to join me in Hawaii so that she could visit Aitken Roshi, a Zen teacher who had greatly inspired her for many years. She met privately with him, and also presented one of the Water Mala bowls and gave a talk to the community there.

Also that year, at the request of my former ICA colleague Dr. Herman Greene, I was an environmental adviser to the Interfaith Conference on Climate Change in New York City.

In September, Bonnie had surgery to remove a noncancerous but serious tumor from the occipital region of her head which had caused her severe pain for the last several years. At last, she would find relief. It was a life-changing surgery. Within a month, she was leading retreats again! Though she would continue to have post-Lyme pain, she was so much better. We were happy beyond words.

In October, I gained much from Gelek Rimpoche's retreat on the Medicine Buddha. I dedicated my participation to Bonnie's full health and the health of the ecosystems of planet Earth.

In mid-January 2011, I got a strong sense that I was called to play a role in helping humanity move through this present and unfolding crisis to a more human and sustainable society. This was not a new idea, but a powerful feeling that I was called to write, speak, organize and facilitate, now, and until I could no longer. Angel Gail had previously told me that "there is a bigger chair for you to sit in after you leave the UN." She did not mean one with more status, but more in alignment with who I was and what I could contribute.

In early February, Bonnie led a beautiful water ceremony, and I gave a keynote address at the Building Creative Communities Conference (BC3) in Colquitt, Georgia. This was at the invitation of an ICA and social artistry colleague Joy Jinks, one of the organizers of the conference and a long-standing leader of her community. Years before, she and her daughter had been short-term volunteers in an ICA village project in Jamaica where I was codirector. It was good to see Jan Sanders, who was teaching social artistry at the conference. Colquitt is famous for its Swamp Gravy theater performances based on community stories and performed each year in Cotton Hall by community residents young and old. All around the small town are huge, stunning murals depicting community stories and values. Every year, Colquitt invited community leaders from around the area and the country to come for training in social artistry and community building.

My talk challenged the participants to respond to this time of crisis and opportunity by building an empathic society, community by community. I shared a number of stories and leadership methods that they could make use of. After my keynote, the Story Bridge founder Dr. Richard Geer took over and led the group in sharing stories, and creating and performing a play-in-a-day. It was incredible how this process built trust and released energy for creative community building. I was sold on the process and on Colquitt.

In April 2011, I traveled back to Kathmandu, Nepal, as a Fulbright Senior Specialist, and designed a master's degree curriculum on training and development. Dr. Tatwa Timsina, founder of ICA Nepal and a professor at Tribhuvan University in Kathmandu, had requested this Fulbright mission. Flying in, the view of the Himalayas was thrilling. Electricity and wifi were off but came back on. I enjoyed staying with Tatwa, his wife, and younger son in their beautiful home. His older son was studying in a US university. To design the curriculum, I met with a group of Nepali professionals, including Dr. Kushendra Mahat and Tatwa. We brainstormed the purpose, categories, methods, and structure of the courses. I then prepared a draft syllabus of the entire curriculum, which the team reviewed and commented on. In the following year, the curriculum appeared in a book published by ICA Nepal, *Changing Lives, Changing Societies*. It was an exciting time being back in Nepal once again. As usual, I visited my favorite Buddhist temple Swayambhunath Stupa in Kathmandu. My vision of the future of Nepal was that it had become the Jewel of the East, facilitating dialogue between China and India, with massive renewable energy, women's full participation, a vibrant democracy, equitable opportunities, a global symbol of peace, and a sustainable environment.

Also that year, I taught two grad courses on innovative leadership at NYU Wagner, first, a five-consecutive-day intensive in May, and then another course in the Fall Semester (September – December) with a traditional fourteen-week format, each class one hour and forty minutes long. I found that stretching the course out and having such short classes did not allow the students to have as intensive an experience as with the weeklong format. One highlight was that at my assignment, each student went to Zuccotti Park in Manhattan, experienced the Occupy Wall Street encampment, and then wrote about it. I also visited the park and was struck that this live-in approach was needed to wake us up to the unjust power structure.

In mid-June, I flew to Dar es Salam, Tanzania. On the way to Mother Africa, the birthplace of the human race, I asked myself: What can I give to Africa and to planet Earth? How can I give voice to the voiceless, to future generations, to the waters, air, soil, plants and animals, and to the poor? Flying over Greece, I thought about its lost grandeur, and wondered if that was a symbol of the future collapse of Western civilization. I found myself thinking about my grandchildren, Phoenix and Mariela. Then, we flew across the Sahara desert just west of the Red Sea, then west of Addis Ababa, remembering that I was first there in 1969, just married, 25 years old.

While in Dar, I gave a keynote address at the UN Public Service Day Awards and Global Forum and facilitated a workshop. Before the forum I had prepared a background paper and trained facilitators. The organizers had given each participant and speaker a colorful batik printed cloth with the UN logo on it. When I gave my keynote, I draped the cloth around one shoulder. Dr. Adriana Alberti of UNDESA had kindly invited me to do this consultancy. It was good to be back in Dar since the time I was there with UNDP several years prior. On my way back to New York, I stopped over in Amsterdam for a few days of looking around with Bonnie, who had flown over to meet me.

In early September, I began teaching the fall course at NYU Wagner, and also helped facilitate the Wisdom Thinkers Network (WTN) meeting in New York City at the suggestion of my former-UNDP colleague Dr. Naresh Singh and the WTN founder, Ralph Singh. It was a deep and wide-ranging discussion. In addition that month, Tatwa and Kushendra spoke at NYU Wagner, at my request, about their work in Nepal.

In October, Jean Houston and Angel Gail once again shared their advice with me. Jean felt that I needed to be writing as a facilitator of change, posing questions so that people could think about what is going on and what is needed. And Angel Gail felt that I needed to feed myself emotionally ("put on your own oxygen mask first, and then help others.") Their suggestions always touched me, although I was often unclear how to implement them.

In New York City in November and December, I facilitated four two-day planning and training workshops for the entire staff of the Division of Public Administration and Development

Management (DPADM)/UNDESA. Previously, I had met with the director a few times, interviewed sixteen staff and designed the workshops. These events were held in Queens in full view of the Manhattan skyline across the East River. The first three workshops were for different units of the division with the final workshop for the directorate. The Chinese director, Qian Haiyan, had asked me at the suggestion of Dr. Adriana Alberti to design and facilitate these workshops in order to help unify her team.

The workshops began with meditation, had group dancing after lunch, and reflection after each session. In each workshop, we used the ICA's Technology of Participation (ToP) strategic planning process. The participants first brainstormed and agreed on their five-year vision for their unit based on their hopes and dreams. Then, they identified and analyzed current obstacles blocking that vision. Next, the participants created strategic directions to deal with the obstacles and move toward their vision. Finally, they created actions plans to implement the strategies in the first year and first quarter, putting the actions on a timeline and deciding the who, what, how, when, and where of each action. DPADM found the workshops energizing and releasing, and the director was pleased that she had a renewed team with which to work.

Because of scheduling and health issues, I declined work that year in Brazil at a UN volunteers conference, and in Jordan with a UN urban conference. After a very full year of work, travel, family, and health challenges, I moved into 2012. As was my custom, I had a vision of the next year, and would prepare monthly, weekly, and daily action plans and what I called reflections-in-action, as I went along.

On January 5, 2012, I had robotic radical prostatectomy performed by Dr. Ashutosh Tewari at New York Presbyterian Hospital. The surgery took place after six months of exploring various treatment options for prostate cancer. My dad had had this type of cancer. Dr. Tewari was a renowned surgeon who had been recommended to me. Before agreeing to this procedure, I had considered many different treatments, both traditional and alternative. Finally, I decided that it would be wise to remove the prostate in this manner. Following the surgery, I recovered at home in Cold Spring, doing a lot of walking to Mozart, and then in February, stayed with Duncan and Lisa in their home in Asheville. At that time, Duncan kindly introduced me to Transcendental Meditation, his life-long preferred meditation technique. It had been difficult to give up my prostate and surrounding tissue, as this had consequences. Later, I would reflect that I would recommend to other men that they explore holistic treatments or CyberKnife. Nevertheless, life went on with this altered body. Of course, I hoped that the cancer would never return. Throughout the journey of this health challenge, I was super-reflective about my life, questioning and analyzing major events, emotions, and decisions. This resulted not so much in new clarity and actions, but rather in a heightened sense of awareness.

In March and April, I continued my healing regimen, and reflected deeply on the many aspects of my suffering, the numerous people and things I loved, and a long list of that for which I was deeply grateful.

Later in May, I traveled to Yogyakarta, Indonesia, made a workshop presentation and provided seminar facilitation for an East-West Center (EWC) Asian regional seminar on local democracy. After the event, I prepared a policy brief. It was great being back in Yogya after many years since I had been there with EI/ICA. My former UNDP colleague Dr. Shabbir Cheema, now head of governance programs at EWC, invited me to help with the seminar. The evening before the seminar, I heard the call to prayer from the Mosque, gamelan music over a dinner of satay, fried noodles, fried rice, carrots, beans, eggplant, corn fritters and fried shrimp, and then saw a Ramayana dance performance. Seminar participants came from eight Asian countries and three others. It was wonderful to hear what was currently happening in democratic institution building around the region. One recurring theme was the battle between oligarchy and democracy.

After the workshop, at sunrise, I visited Borobudur, the world's largest Buddhist temple, with a former UNDP consultant, Myo Myint. Myo, originally from Myanmar, had lived with his wife and daughter in New York City, where he graduated from Columbia University graduate schools. When he traveled back to Myanmar to see his sick mother, he was not allowed reentry into the US because of a visa issue. He then spent several years living and working in Singapore separated from his family in New York. When he visited my hotel, I cried when I met him, so filled with sadness at his family separation. Borobudur at sunrise was awe inspiring.

In June, I made a keynote and workshop presentation in the UN Public Service Day Awards and Global Forum in New York City at the invitation of UNDESA.

In July, I was saddened that Jim O'Neill, Jennifer's wonderful dad, and my grandkids' other grandpa, passed away.

In September, I taught Innovative Leadership for Sustainable Development for my fifth year at NYU Wagner. I tried a new format, teaching one full Saturday five weeks in a row. I found this to have the advantages of intensity for the students along with more time for reading and preparing assignments. Columbia University Professor Kathy Callahan was again a guest teacher in the section on systems change. She spoke about her experience within the EPA when she was a senior official. Sean Southey, executive director of the nonprofit PCI Media in New York City, spoke in the cultural change section about the importance of using stories to change people's views and behaviors. Austin Aigbe, an A student from Nigeria with an International Ford Foundation fellowship, returned to his country after graduation and became a senior staff member of the Center for Democracy and Development. Another top student in the class, Maureen Connally, a genius at event planning turned innovations planner, later was to help the UN prepare for its 75th anniversary program. Also that semester, I became a Senior Fellow of the NYU Research Center for Leadership in Action at NYU Wagner.

My 2012 NYU Wagner class

In late October-early November, I gave a keynote address for the ICA International's global conference on human development held in Kathmandu, Nepal. It was meaningful being back in Nepal for my sixth visit since 1969. Dr. Timsina had invited me to make the keynote. He circulated at the conference a book, *Changing Lives, Changing Societies,* that had recently been published by ICA Nepal. I was happy to have written two of the chapters in the book, one co-authored with Tatwa. Again, I visited and circumambulated my special Buddhist temple in Kathmandu, Swayambhunath Stupa.

In New York City in December, I facilitated a DPADM/UNDESA three-day annual strategic planning retreat. Before the event, I trained in-house facilitators, and prepared a background paper. I was proud of the DPADM staff whom I had trained and who did a great job facilitating their first working groups.

After spending January – March 2013, in Asheville, as usual, writing and with family, we returned to New York. Then, in April, I met with NYU Wagner's Research Center for Leadership in Action, UN Women, and my doctors; and Bonnie gave weekly talks at the Japan Society. I experienced a sudden relief and comfort knowing that even if my species doesn't make it due to our own greed and delusion, that life on Earth and throughout the cosmos will continue to unfold over the next several billion years. But, oh, how I would love for us humans to continue our journey! I vowed that I would do all within my power toward that end.

I was blessed in May to attend another retreat with Gelek Rimpoche at the Garrison Institute.

In June that year, I traveled for the first time to Manama, the capital of Bahrain, a desert island nation between Saudi Arabia and Qatar. There I made a plenary presentation on participatory governance to 600 government and NGO officials from around the world in the UN Global Forum on Public Service (the presentation is on the UNDESA website). After that, I helped design and participate in the forum's UN Expert Group Meeting on e-government. One of the unusual events during the workshop was a dinner hosted by the king at his palace in Manama. A treat after the meeting was getting to drive a go-cart on the big track dressed in racing suit and helmet. I was proud of myself even though I didn't win. I survived, and that was sufficient.

Giving a keynote address at the UN global forum in Manama, Bahrain

Bonnie and I attended in early July a family reunion on Whidbey Island near Seattle celebrating the fiftieth wedding anniversary of Marjorie and John Bachert, my sister-in-law and brother-in-law. It was fun being there with Bonnie, both sons, Jennifer, and our grandchildren, as well as many other relatives and friends. It was delightful to be back in John and Marjorie's beautiful, three-acre garden that they designed, planted, and cared for, especially the small memorial garden at the bottom of the kettle with pond and a Kwan Yin statute in honor of Mary, Marjorie's sister.

Also in July, in New York City, I taught in the NYU Research Center for Leadership in Action's Global Social Change Leadership Institute. I also advised former NYU grad students on their careers and further graduate study.

I was delighted to write a cover endorsement for my former UNDP colleague Dr. G. Shabbir Cheema's new book on *Local Democracy in Asia* published by UN University. The book was based on papers he commissioned at the East-West Center in Honolulu.

On September 2, Bonnie and I celebrated our sixth wedding anniversary. I enjoyed having lunch regularly with my oldest son, Benjamin, in New York. Bonnie and I spent winter and summer in Asheville, as usual, near grandson Phoenix and granddaughter Mariela, my son Christopher, daughter-in-law Jennifer, brother Duncan, sister-in-law Lisa, and friends. It was a lot of driving back and forth, but it was worth it.

22

BLOGGING, POLITICAL ACTIVISM, BOOK WRITING, AND MORE: Cold Spring, NY; Garrison, NY; New York City; Swannanoa, NC; and planet Earth

On September 22, 2013, I inaugurated *A Compassionate Civilization* blog site (https://compassionatecivilization.blogspot.com/) and published 56 posts over the next three months. This writing seemed to download rapidly from my heart-mind, almost one post per day. I was excited and motivated to create these posts and felt that I was sharing valuable ideas related to both the crises humanity faces and the strategies and actions needed to address them. In addition to writing new posts, I made use of excerpts of my NYU lectures, UN keynotes, poetry, and autobiographical material.

In October, I began teaching two grad courses at NYU Wagner. The first was Innovative Leadership for Sustainable Human Development taught on the five consecutive Saturdays format. In addition, I taught for the first time a grad course on International

Capstone. Capstone was one of the final requirements for Wagner students before they received their master's degree. In small teams for nine months (fall of one year until summer of the next), they acted as consultants to an organization assisting it in addressing a real issue of planning, research, design, evaluation, or management. My student teams were working with two UN agencies, UNDESA and UNESCO. The UNESCO team conducted its initial meetings with the agency, did some research, and then traveled to Paris for an orientation at UNESCO HQ, and then on to Freetown, Sierra Leone, to help design and facilitate a Local Scoping Exercise on futures and foresight. Students always learned on many levels from this experiential exercise.

And with PCI Media, a global NGO in New York City, I facilitated in October a workshop helping them create their organizational song, story, and symbol. I then attended a 350. org rally in New York City on climate chaos mitigation with Bill McKibben. I met with colleagues from Canada, the US, and Argentina regarding a north-south leadership project, and provided advice to Jan Sanders on the design of a one-year leadership course at the University of Aruba. I advised Trusted Sharing, an internet startup designed by my brother, Duncan, formerly the chief scientist for LinkedIn. And I posted regularly on social media.

I traveled to Nairobi, Kenya, in late October-early November, as a consultant with a UN Habitat land tenure global program for the poor. While there, I facilitated a staff workshop and attended a capacity development strategy briefing. Colleague Lowie Rosales-Kawasaki had told the team about my work in facilitation and governance, and I was asked to be their consultant for this initiative. This was the first of two visits to Nairobi for this work. The city was filled with brilliant blue jacaranda trees. There was an air of apprehension in the city because of recent terrorist attacks that killed several people in a mall. I had reflected on the possibility of new attacks and decided to go anyway.

Back in the US, I worked out in the gym three times a week, maintained a healthy diet, and continued regular reading, daily meditation, mantras and journal writing. I was committed to taking care of myself so that I could care for others.

In January 2014, I returned to Nairobi, Kenya, for the next phase of my four-month organizational development consultancy with UN Habitat's global program on land access for the poor. I helped the team create a new organizational design, reporting lines, priorities, partnerships, staffing transitions, and a strategic plan.

In March, at Oklahoma City University (OCU) I made a keynote presentation at the invitation of Rev. Dr. Mark Davies, OCU dean of arts and sciences, in a symposium on creative peacemaking. My topic was the "Four Faces of War and Peace." I based the talk on Ken Wilber's quadrants of mindsets, behaviors, cultures, and systems. The participants actively dialogued with each other and seemed to appreciate the presentation. (Video is on the internet.) It was great being back on the Oklahoma prairie once again. My brother, Duncan, had flown out from Asheville with me, and his son Matthew, from Fairfield, Iowa, met us there for the event. Other ICA colleagues from Oklahoma and north Texas were present.

Also in March, at the University of Aruba (UA), I taught with Jan Sanders at her invitation and with UA's Dr. Juliet Chieuw in a seminar on collaborative leadership for educational administrators. Juliet was head of UA's quality management and an awesome tai chi master. I made a presentation on our critical times and helped facilitate a strategic planning workshop. Aruba, part of the ABC (Aruba, Bonaire, Curacao) islands, was just off the northern coast of Venezuela. When I lived in Caracas, I had been to Curacao a couple of times, once to facilitate a strategic planning workshop for a bank, and another time with Benjamin to get a visa extension. Being in tiny Aruba was fascinating—a tropical paradise of wind and waves. One highlight was meeting

Dr. Glenn Thode, the rector of UA who had written about Aruba becoming an enlightened society with the help of the university. I wrote a blog post about this.

Facilitating a strategic planning workshop with the
University of Aruba class on collaborative leadership

In North Carolina, we learned that we had to leave our beloved cabin because the owners wanted to occupy it. We were sad about leaving. After many conversations, we decided that we were ready to commit to North Carolina as where we would eventually land full-time, and that it was time to buy rather than rent again. In April, Bonnie and I bought a house in Swannanoa, ten minutes from East Asheville, to be near children and grandchildren. We looked at many houses; and Bonnie found a house on a hillside that we both liked not too far from our old cabin, We named it Chickadee Cottage. It was surrounded by woods on three sides. We did some renovation, during which we could not live in the house for a few months. For that time period, we stayed at the kind invitation of Duncan and Lisa, in a cottage on their property in Asheville. It was one of four cottages built near their house that Lisa had designed and supervised the construction. The renovation process of our house was very stressful for both Bonnie and me.

Also that year at NYU Wagner, I taught two courses, one on International Strategic Management and the International Capstone (with my students assisting UNDESA and UNESCO) that I had begun in the fall of the previous year. The Capstone course ended in May with presentations to the client organizations, to our class, and a live exhibition on campus of all of the Capstone projects. This was the first time I taught International Strategic Management. The format was one full Saturday five weeks in a row during the fall semester. In the first class, we focused on our critical moment of crisis and opportunity. In the remaining four classes, I introduced, demonstrated, and enabled students to experience the ICA ToP strategic planning process and workshop method: discerning a practical vision; identifying current obstacles; designing strategic directions; and creating action plans and timelines. When we arrived at the final session on action planning, the students realized how the previous three workshops had been utterly necessary to provide solid results and follow-up.

At the invitation of Dr. Adriana Alberti, in June, I facilitated a workshop in Seoul, South Korea, on e-governance and made a presentation at the global UN Forum on Public Service and Sustainable Development. My talk was about collaborative governance and is on the internet. After the UN conference in Seoul, I had a wonderful reunion with dear friends. Rev. Dr. Kang Byoung Hoon came to my hotel for a meal and conversation. I attended a church service at Bo Moon Methodist Church in Seoul, where Rev. Dr. Park Si Won's son Rev. Park Chul Hyun is pastor. There I got to meet Park So Hyun, Rev. Park's daughter who is a famous, German-trained organist and music professor, and the lovely grandchildren of Rev. Park and his wife Mrs. Lee Jung Ja. Rev. Park and his son also drove me out to Kuh Du I Ri, a village just south of the demilitarized zone, where his family and mine had conducted a village development project in the ICA days. The village was totally transformed as is all of Korea—so many wonderful memories.

In July, I participated in the NYU Wagner Leadership Initiative Community of Practice, taught a session on international development for Ghanaian women leaders, and made a presentation on decentralized governance to Albanian urban planners visiting NYU Wagner. And I was invited to teach Organizational and Managerial Development, and Project Management at NYU Wagner in the coming year. I was really enjoying being a grad school prof.

On my blog site *A Compassionate Civilization* I published 45 posts; and *Kosmos Journal* published my article on "The Movement of Movements." The ICA newsletter *Wind and Waves* published my article on my mission to and reflections on South Korea, and I continued posting on Facebook, LinkedIn and Twitter. In addition, I continued advising the new social media startup Trusted Sharing that my brother was developing.

At Warren Wilson College (WWC), near our house in Swannanoa, I made a presentation at the invitation of Professor Amy Knisley to some of her environmental students and interested faculty on "The Future of Life on Earth: Utopia or Dystopia?" WWC is an excellent, small liberal arts school based on three pillars—study, work on campus, and community service. The college also hosts annual folk and chamber music festivals and has an excellent writing program.

I was privileged that year to love and care for my spouse, Bonnie, two sons and daughter-in-law. I enjoyed living six months of the year near six-year-old grandson, Phoenix, and four-year-old granddaughter Mariela in Asheville and communed with my brother, Duncan, and sister-in-law Lisa in Asheville. I met with Work cousins PK and Susan in Oklahoma City. And I celebrated my son Christopher's fortieth birthday and my seventieth. Time, it was a fleeting.

That year I visited good friends in Asheville and met with dear friends in New York, where we lived half the year. And I stayed in touch with friends around the world by phone and email. To care for my health, I worked out in a gym three times per week both in New York and North Carolina, ate mostly vegetables and fish, took supplements, meditated, read, relaxed, and rested.

I was grateful for my life that year and for the opportunity to serve others on this beautiful planet. With so much suffering and so many challenges facing humanity, my wish for 2015 was for peace, happiness, compassion, and understanding for all people and all beings everywhere. I wished that it would be so!

In 2015, at NYU Wagner, I taught four courses: International Capstone in April-May, Organizational and Managerial Development (OMD) in April-May, and Project Management (PM) in June and again in the fall semester. This was the first time I taught OMD and PM. OMD was in a five-Saturday format with sessions on our critical times, challenges, culture and values, barriers to success, and action planning. Christina Feng (now Collette), one of my A students, was IT project leader at New York Presbyterian Hospital and is now also a leadership and career coach. PM was a two-credit-hour course on the "PIE" process— project Planning, Implementation, and Evaluation. Students loved using Trusted Sharing (TS) online to get to know each other before the first class and then to work together in teams throughout the course. I used TS in all my courses.

Also that year, I designed, by request of the head of the Management section, a project management module for the Capstone faculty. I also participated in the leadership community of practice (CoP) meetings and shared my experience with international students. In all of my courses, I wove into the existing curriculum the methods, models, and contexts that I knew were effective and needed. These included an introductory context on the critical times in which we are living, a vision of a compassionate civilization, and methods of ICA's Technology of Participation (ToP), Jean Houston's social artistry, and Ken Wilber's integral frameworks. Required readings included ICA-related books such as *The Art of Focused Conversations, More than 50 Ways to Build Team Consensus, The Facilitative Way, The Workshop Book,* and *Transformative Strategies.*

In October at Horace Mann (HM), an elite private school in New York City, I gave a lecture and workshop to its very bright students, dedicated faculty, and devoted parents on global citizenship, visionary leadership, and sustainable development. This was at the invitation of social artistry colleague Karen Johnson, photography teacher at HM.

I continued testing, promoting, and advising Trusted Sharing (TS) by designing and facilitating online, flextime conversations, developing case studies and introducing TS, in addition to NYU, to ICAI, IAF and the UN. I continued publishing blog posts on *A Compassionate Civilization,* comments on Facebook, LinkedIn, Twitter and Google+, an article in ICAI's *Wind and Waves* e-magazine, and blog posts in the *Social Artist's e-Companion* at the invitation of publisher Joyce McNamara. For the Fulbright Specialist Program, I acted as a peer reviewer for applications from local governance specialists wishing to assist institutions of higher learning in other countries.

At the invitation of UNDP, I attended the world premiere at the Ford Foundation in New York City of a film on climate change. I also stayed in touch with my friends who were current or previous UN staff stationed in or visiting New York City and celebrated the UN's seventieth anniversary and the launch of the UN's seventeen sustainable development goals (SDGs) for 2030.

UN Sustainable Development Goals for 2030: UN SDG website: https://www.un.org/sustainabledevelopment/ The content of this publication has not been approved by the UN and does not reflect the views of the UN or its officials or Member States.

On the personal and family side, I continued daily meditation and thrice-weekly workouts in gyms in New York and North Carolina, traveled to Chicago with Bonnie to celebrate our wedding anniversary, and the wedding reception of my dear friends Bruce Williams and Jack Wallace. Bruce, who is in his late 70s, had been spending half his time in China training principals and teachers in group facilitation. I had many years earlier worked with Bruce in Korea with the ICA. Bonnie and I hosted our two grandkids' first sleepover at Chickadee Cottage. Sadly, that year, my dear aunt Hiahwahnah Work passed away at 95, along with three dear colleagues – Mary Ann Wainwright, Marielena Granger, and Lela Jahn. And our dear cat Squirrel died.

In order to reduce our budget, Bonnie and I moved our New York home in December from our Cold Spring apartment to the old Sexton's Cottage on the campus of St. Peter's Episcopal Church in neighboring Garrison. We missed being on the riverfront in Cold Spring, but we loved the big trees, dramatic ice age rock formations, and the old cemetery at St. Philip's. We named our home Outcrop Cottage. We were near the Metro-North train station, the Hudson Highlands, and our former home on Route 9D—such a gorgeous area of trees, hills, and river.

My intention for the next year was to focus on climate activism, supporting the election of Democratic Party candidates, writing, publishing, advising, teaching, and consulting. I wished that all beings everywhere might realize peace, happiness, compassion, and understanding!

In 2016 at NYU Wagner, I taught forty-six international and national grad students in two courses—Organizational and Managerial Development in April, and Strategic Management in September-October—and participated in the NYU Leadership Community of Practice. The teamwork and the class presentations were always highlights for the students and for me.

My NYU Wagner Strategic Management class 2016

In April, I provided consulting services of designing and

facilitating a workshop for the UN Task Team, and editing a global urban declaration in preparation for the UN Habitat III global conference on sustainable urban development. In October, I provided consulting services along with my consulting partner Dr. Cosmas Gitta related to three case studies to the UNDP/ University of Aruba Center of Excellence on Sustainable Development for the Small Island Developing States. I advised Trusted Sharing (TS), a social media startup, including designing and facilitating a TS staff retreat in March and designing and facilitating several online, flextime TS conversations for my NYU students. I prepared for publication manuscripts on a compassionate civilization, and on decentralizing governance. I shared the first one with David Marshall, Vice President at BK publishing, for his helpful advice and the second with NYU publishing.

During that year in my personal and family life, I made phone calls to get out the vote, canvassed and donated to Bernie Sanders's primary campaign and the Hillary Clinton general election campaign. I also signed petitions and called government officials to oppose the policies and appointments of the president-elect. I donated to various social causes and charities. I wrote daily on social media. Bonnie and I continued to live in both New York and North Carolina. We held overnight Chickadee Camp for the grandkids at our home. We celebrated the completed life of our beloved dog Lady on September 1 and welcomed our new kitten, Mr. Chickabee (yes, not Chickadee). I continued thrice-weekly exercise at gyms in New York and North Carolina, and daily journaling and meditation—self-care for world care. I struggled with doubt concerning my life's impact and uncertainties that lay ahead.

*"GrandBonnie" (her favorite name) with her two
grandchildren, Phoenix and Mariela*

As with many people, I was shocked and appalled that the US general election concluded as it did. That night I went into AFib. The stress and despair were too great for my heart to keep its normal rhythm.

I was grateful for my life and work that year. I continued to explore and learn. I rededicated my work and life to making a difference for people and planet in 2017. This was to include writing/publishing, activism, teaching, consulting, advising, loving my family, and caring for my mind and body.

I declared at the end of the year: Onward toward a compassionate civilization moment by moment!

Bonnie's beautiful work with Hermitage Heart had continued over these years in spite of the times she had her disabling head pain and post-Lyme fibromyalgia. In Garrison, Hermitage Heart had rented a charming gristmill on a stream that became a home for meditation and retreats. The Water Mala initiative that she created had provided deep contemplation of the mystery of the life-giving nature of water. The ritual included 108 handmade ceramic bowls arranged like a mala each filled with water—the number 108 signifying the infinite. Bonnie published two books of her profound dharma talks, *Winter Moon* and *Empty Branches*. She taught for several years on a weekly basis at the Japan Society in New York City, with new and old students coming from the city as well as the surrounding area. She gave the keynote address at the thirty-fifth anniversary of her monastery. Even though I was not her student, I loved to attend her meditations and talks and help her prepare for her events. Her ability to present subtle truth through personal and traditional Zen stories always touched me. I must confess that I was proud of her.

In fact, I was proud of everyone in my family. Benjamin had been a highly responsible manager and worker, owned his own apartment, and loved his family, especially his niece and nephew, it would appear from his frequent visits to Asheville. Christopher was a valued senior IT expert at a multinational corporation and a devoted father, husband, son, and brother. Jennifer was a super-responsible mother, friend to many, and artistic craftsperson. Phoenix and Mariela were so very bright, kind, and creative, inventing new world's with their fertile imaginations. Kathy, Jennifer's mother who lives with them, was a master chef, artist, and devoted nana to her grandchildren. Duncan was a genius at online innovation and deeply concerned about enhancing societal dialogue in a time of increasing polarization. Lisa was a home schooling practitioner, an untiring organizer, designer, family historian, and much more. And Matthew and Kesha were brilliant thinkers and project organizers, among much else. How fortunate I was to be journeying with this family of good, talented, caring people.

Christopher, Phoenix, Jennifer, and Mariela

2017 was a year of highs and lows, births and deaths, dangers and opportunities, despair and hope. After ten years of teaching at NYU Wagner as adjunct professor of innovative leadership, because of my relocation to North Carolina, I taught my last Wagner course that year on organizational and managerial development in April-May. I had so enjoyed working with the many caring students dedicated to public service from around the country and the world and collaborating with other faculty members. I knew I would miss Washington Square, the students, and teaching.

I focused much energy in April-July on editing my manuscript of *A Compassionate Civilization*, working with CreateSpace on its editing, and interior and cover design, and creating a detailed marketing plan. It was hard work but exciting to do all of this because I so believed in its messages and because of my love of language and books. I felt as though I was coming into my own as a writer, even though I had already helped UNDP write and publish several books. And it was enlivening to realize that I was married to an author. We would be hermit writers together.

Cosmas and I helped prepare two more case studies for UNDP's Center of Excellence on Sustainable Development in Small Island Developing States.

I joined the local Democratic Party precinct in Swannanoa and attended meetings of Our Revolution in Asheville. In January, I attended a Buddhist retreat near Oklahoma City led by Drs. Larry Ward and Peggy Rowe Ward and met in Oklahoma City with my cousins PK and Susan Work, her daughter Kelli Brooke Haney, and Professor Mark Davies of Oklahoma City University. In New York, I met with old friends, Rev. Dr. Kang Byoung Hoon and his daughter Rev. Dr. Kang Hye Kyung. Bonnie and I held more sleepovers at Chickadee Cottage in Swannanoa for the grandkids, and we enjoyed hosting dear friends Lowie, Wataru, and Megumi (our honorary granddaughter) Kawasaki in our home in Garrison.

There were many highlights during this eleven-year life phase (mid-2006-mid-2017) of consulting, teaching, speaking, writing on social media, and engaging in activism. I had married an incredible human being, Bonnie Myotai Treace. As an adjunct professor of innovative leadership, I taught many bright, caring students from several countries over a ten-year period at NYU Wagner Graduate School of Public Service teaching the official curriculum of five different courses and sharing my UNDP and ICA methods, models, experiences, and passion. I became a grandfather of two beautiful grandchildren, Phoenix Orion Work and Mariela Katherine Work, and was helping them grow up as they were helping me grow older. I consulted with several international organizations, including the East-West Center, UNDESA, and UN Habitat, introducing new ideas of integral thinking and social artistry, methods of facilitation, and a passion for transformation. I gave keynote presentations in a number of UN and other conferences around the world, challenging people to wake up to the climate/justice crises of the twenty-first century and to take the actions required. I launched my blog on a compassionate civilization, providing a vision of a hoped-for future for humanity and practical recommendations on the mindful activism needed. I also worked on the manuscript for the soon-to-be-published book *A Compassionate Civilization* that would launch my next life phase.

I felt that I was about to enter yet another adventure of my life and work and was ready to jump into the unknown once again.

PART FIVE

CATALYZING A COMPASSIONATE-ECOLOGICAL CIVILIZATION, WHILE AGING ACTIVELY

Being an author, climate/justice activist, and founder of Compassionate Civilization Collaborative [C3] (with a bit of facilitation and public speaking): mid 2017 – 2019, and beyond, 73 – 75 – ?, based in Swannanoa, NC

In August 2017, Nepal's parliament banned menstruation huts, effective the next year. Genetic study of the apple revealed its origin was in Kazakhstan. Barack Obama's tweet "no one is born hating another person because of the color of his skin or his background or his religion" in response to the Charlottesville violence, became the most liked tweet ever.

> "Our house is on fire. I am here to say, our house is on fire. [...] I want you to act as you would in a crisis. I want you to act as if our house is on fire. Because it is."
> -Greta Thunberg

23

BOOK PUBLISHED, AND ITS MESSAGES SPREAD FAR AND WIDE: Swannanoa, NC; Garrison, NY; planet Earth

On August 1, 2017, the day after my 73rd birthday, my book was published and I began marketing *A Compassionate Civilization: The Urgency of Sustainable Development and Mindful Activism – Reflections and Recommendations.* (https://www.amazon.com/dp/1546972617) This book was my declaration to the world and contained the messages I felt were essential to be promoted and acted upon.

In summary, the book proclaimed that: "We live in the most critical time in human history. We face interlocking crises of climate chaos, patriarchy, systemic poverty, plutocracy, bigotry, and perpetual warfare. Let us dare to dream and realize a new civilization of compassion. Let us take the necessary actions for environmental sustainability, gender equality, socioeconomic justice, participatory governance, cultural tolerance, and nonviolence and peace. Let us work together to do all of this as a movement of movements (MOM.) Let us do this as mindful activists using methods of innovative leadership including participatory facilitation, integral frameworks, and social artistry. Let us do this as global-local citizens. And let us do this while cultivating understanding and compassion, realizing happiness, celebrating gratitude, living lifelong commitment, choosing courage, dancing with time, and embracing sadness, sickness, old age, and death."

Author at Barnes & Noble in Asheville, North Carolina

My intention was not only to publish and market this book but to promote its important messages and encourage the necessary actions in every way I could, through presentations, interviews, videos, articles, excerpts, podcasts, websites, online study groups, and more.

After celebrating with Bonnie our tenth wedding anniversary on September 2, I traveled to Oklahoma State University (OSU) for a fiftieth anniversary of campus activists. There, I spoke to a sociology class about my book and signed copies, and also signed copies for my fellow/sister activists. The OSU Student Union put copies of my book in the store. It was wonderful being back on the prairie at my alma mater with so many colleagues and memories. Returning to OSU was a pilgrimage to the beginning of my journey of world service. In fact, the first time I was at OSU (then Oklahoma A & M), I was four years old and my dad was getting his master's degree on the GI Bill. After the reunion, I was happy to visit my wonderful first cousin PK and her amazing wife, Melissa, in their home in Stillwater.

For the first time in my life I was no longer part of an institution as my missional vehicle as ICA, UNDP, or NYU had been for fifty years. I was now an independent and interdependent published author and climate/justice activist preparing to be based full time in North Carolina. A new era had dawned once again.

Articles about and excerpts of *A Compassionate Civilization* appeared on the NYU Wagner website, ICA International website, Garrison Institute website, Foundation of Global Governance and Sustainability website, Stillwater, Oklahoma, newspaper, *Highlands Current* newspaper in New York, *O Globo* Portuguese-language newspaper in Brazil, and the CP Yen Foundation Chinese-language newsletter. The book could be ordered from Amazon, IngramSpark, Barnes & Noble, NYU bookstore in New York City, Malaprop's bookstore in Asheville, North Carolina, and OSU student union in Stillwater Oklahoma. Author readings and signings took place in the Garrison, New York, library, and ICA USA GreenRise in Chicago at the ICA Archives meeting. Facebook pages were created for *A Compassionate Civilization*, and for the Movement of Movements (MOM.) A seven-session online book study took place, kindly facilitated by Kathy McGrane and her colleagues. And I initiated the Compassionate Civilization Collaborative (C3) to help strengthen the movement of movements (MOM.) Endorsements for the book were gratefully received from Dr. Shabbir Cheema, Dr. Jean Houston, Dr. Terry Bergdall, Joy Jinks, Dr. Larry Ward, Nancy Roof, Bruce Williams and Dr. Tatwa Timsina.

In 2018, I spoke about my book to the Creative Facilitators' Meetup in Asheville. I was interviewed on three radio programs, each producing a podcast on the internet: *Speaking of Travel* based in Asheville, invited by host Marilyn Ball; *Glocal News of Social Artistry* in Missouri, invited by host Dr. Dick Dalton; and twice on *Democratic Perspectives* in Arizona, invited by host Stephen

Williamson a former Mystery School colleague. At the invitation of Dr. Justin Whitaker, I was interviewed on the Buddhadoor website, with book excerpts on the American Buddhist Perspectives, and Progressive Buddhism websites. Bonnie and I participated in the Barnes & Noble authors festival in the Asheville Mall, sharing a table and signing our books. BookAuthority recognized my book as an outstanding work on social activism. I raised funds for the Nepali language edition of *ACC*. Former ICA colleague, Buddhist practitioner, great writer, and sister Okie, Pat Webb, wrote a book review of *ACC* that was published in the Thich Nhat Hanh journal *The Mindfulness Bell.* We were getting the word out!

Bonnie Myotai Treace (and me) signing our books at
Barnes & Noble in Asheville, North Carolina

And yet at one point I reflected that: "I am so stressed by the insanity happening to my country and world. What can I do to help? Nothing is enough – a book, a project, an organization, an action, a word, a thought, a feeling – nothing seems powerful enough to change the world. What has changed the world? On the other hand, everything changes the world, every person, every word, every action, every book, every thought, every organization. So it is up to each person, up to me in this case, to act, to write, to speak, to join, to organize, to love, and to die. That is all we, I, can do."

I sent the book to the Philadelphia Library Exhibition. At the invitation of Francielle Lacle of the Center of Excellence on Sustainability for Small Island Developing States (SIDS) based in Aruba, I discussed the book by Skype with the youthful Aruba Global Shapers of the World Economic Forum. I sent book flyers to the International Association of Facilitators (IAF) of North American conference in western Canada. (Several years ago, the ICA had helped establish the IAF.) I participated in an online webinar on the ToP methods written about in my book led by master facilitators Martin Gilbraith and Sunny Walker. I mailed copies of the book to Senator Bernie Sanders, Bill Moyers, and David Korten, and heard from them. There were now 25 endorsements and reviews for the book. New ones, in addition to those published in the book, were written by Dr. Thomas Jay Oord, Ken Fisher, Chic Dambach, Patricia Webb, Rose Ann Sands, Jim Troxel, Jack Gilles, Kaze Gadway, Dr. Cosmas Gitta, Karen Bueno, George Holcombe, Dr. Monica Sharma, Larry Philbrook, Dr. Dick Dalton, Judi White, Dr. Harold Nelson, and Karen Johnson.

In September, I promoted the messages of *A Compassionate Civilization* by giving the keynote address on the International Day of Peace at the World Fair Field Festival and Symposium in Fairfield, Iowa. My nephew Matthew Lindberg-Work had told the World Fair Field organizers, Kaye Jacobs and Richard Beall, leaders of a private school at the Maharishi University of Management (MUM), about my UN career and my new book, and the organizers invited me to give the keynote. I had been in Fairfield several years prior when my nephew had received his undergraduate degree from the Maharishi University. Matthew had then taught chemistry at MUM. Duncan and Lisa visited Fairfield whenever they could, as they were both trained Transcendental

Meditation (TM) teachers and practitioners. I enjoyed being back in Fairfield, meeting so many fine people and participating in the symposium and the festival in the town square. People were very kind throughout my stay there. And I got to meet Kesha Nelson, Matthew's fiancée. What a great lady. Welcome to the family, Kesha! Later, I commissioned a "Compassionate Communities" video produced by Werner Elmker based on the film he took of my keynote in Fairfield. (It is on the internet.)

One day, I reflected that "the NYU bookstore in NYC put the book in the political science section. Barnes & Noble in Peekskill, NY, put it in philosophy. Malaprops in Asheville, NC, put it in current events. Barnes & Noble in the Asheville Mall put it in the spirituality section. The OSU bookstore put it at the front entrance. This all makes sense. It is a collection of different perspectives on a compassionate civilization. There are also speeches, poetry and autobiography in it. It seems right to be multi-perspective. It also includes Ken Wilber's integral quadrants, the ICA's ToP strategic planning process, the UN's sustainable development goals (SDGs), and more. It is an art form, a collage. It is architectural. It is a symphony. It is a handbook. It is a revelation. It is a toolkit. It is visionary. It is about leadership. It is about taking care of yourself."

I also helped prepare, along with my consulting partner Dr. Cosmas Gitta, two more case studies for the UNDP Center of Excellence in Aruba on Small Island Developing States (SIDS)—one on renewable energy in Jeju, Republic of Korea, and another on agritourism in Grenada. UNDP's Emergency Response office put me on their roster of consultants. I spoke to a class at Lenoir Rhyne University in Asheville. And I volunteered with the Democratic Party to get out the vote in the midterm elections.

One day that year, I wrote that: "We do not live on Earth. We are the Earth. We are Earth-air breathers, Earth-water drinkers, Earth-plant and animal eaters, Earth-soil dwellers and tillers, Earth-mountain viewers, Earth-sea sailors, Earth-sky flyers. We have evolved as part of Earth for thousands, millions, billions of years. We are Earth's children and stewards. Why then have we become Earth destroyers, Earth polluters? We have lost our way. We think that we are Earth conquerors, but we are sadly wrong. As Earth-ice melts, seas rise, storms slam, droughts hit, crops die, we and all Earth-creatures will suffer and die. Wake up, wake up! Protect the Earth, our Mother."

For various reasons, I declined kind invitations to speak at UN conferences in South Korea and in Morocco and to conduct a workshop at the Parliament of World Religions meeting in Canada. In August, I was saddened by the death of Kofi Annan, former UN Secretary-General. I was excited to begin preparing manuscripts of my poetry and essays for publication.

Son Benjamin (middle) with dear friends Rev. Dr. Park Si Won (left)
and Rev. Dr. Kang Byoung Hoon (right) during Benjamin's visit to
Seoul, December 2017. I had planned to be with him but didn't go.

In service to family and self, Bonnie and I closed Outcrop Cottage in Garrison, New York, moved some items, and on May 1, established a single home at Chickadee Cottage in Swannanoa, North Carolina. There would henceforth be no more bilocating and driving back and forth twice a year! Before that, Bonnie and I visited friends Lowie, Wataru, and Megumi Kawasaki in New York City; we welcomed Abby the collie into our family; and I participated in daily meditation at another wonderful mindfulness retreat near Oklahoma City with Drs. Larry and Peggy Rowe Ward of the Order of Interbeing. I attended some of grandson Phoenix's exciting soccer matches. I worked out in the gym each week and also got my first hearing aid. Bonnie, the grandkids, and I created our cottage garden in the front of Chickadee Cottage with a flagstone walkway, gate, flowers, bushes and trees. I welcomed former ICA colleague Dr. Herman Greene back for a visit, including to some of Climate City's (Asheville) climate-related attractions, including The Collider, a climate enterprise incubator. I helped Bonnie host family dinners at our house, including Christmas Eve. And Bonnie and I attended special events at the grandkids's Waldorf school, Sacred Mountain. Bonnie rented a space in Asheville to lead meditation and then moved the zendo to nearby Black Mountain. She was contracted to write another book (*Wake Up!*) that was scheduled to appear in October 2019.

In December, I realized that I was drawn more and more to writing my autobiography in 2019. This would allow me to gestalt my memories, feelings, stories, and resolves into a public story that might be helpful to others. I would also be clear concerning what I have to do before I leave this incarnation. To do this I would need to prepare the space, prepare my mind, create a draft, edit, and publish.

I was deeply grateful for 2018 and looked forward to the coming of a year of new possibilities and service. My community and world priorities for 2019 were to be an author and activist promoting compassionate, just, and sustainable development, as well as to do a little consulting and public speaking. My 2019 priorities for family were to care for each family member and my body-mind-spirit.

In January 2019, the Nepali-language edition of *A Compassionate Civilization (ACC)* was launched. When the book had been published in English in August 2017, Dr. Tatwa Timsina, professor, author, and founder of ICA Nepal, read it and felt that it was highly relevant for his country. ICA Nepal then translated, printed, and distributed the book. Copies were given to each member of parliament, with a study group formed, to each cabinet minister, and to each provincial chief, as well as put on the Kathmandu market. May it serve the beautiful people and land of a compassionate Nepal.

Drs. Kushendra Mahat and Tatwa Timsina presenting Nepali edition of ACC to the Minister of Province 1 of Nepal

Also in late January and early February, I returned to Colquitt, Georgia, to the Building Creative Communities Conference and gave a keynote address on creating a compassionate community and civilization and a workshop on discerning your life story. It was wonderful being back in magical Colquitt, the home of Swamp Gravy, especially being with colleagues Joy Jinks, Jan Sanders, and Richard Sims. Again, I experienced the transformative power of the Story Bridge process of a play-in-a-day (PIAD), generating community trust and energy for community development. Dr. Qinghong Wei, executive director of Story Bridge, and Dr. Richard Geer, its founder, proposed partnering with me in future storytelling, planning, and training events based on my book, their process, and my methods of planning and training. I happily agreed.

I mailed copies of *A Compassionate Civilization* to US House Representative Alexandria Ocasio-Cortez of New York (popularly known as AOC), and Daniel Christian Wahl, PhD.

I helped prepare two more sustainable development case studies along with Dr. Cosmas Gitta for the UNDP Center of Excellence based in Aruba.

I continued working on a Compassionate Civilization Collaborative (C3) to strengthen the movement of movements (MOM) through online communication, interchange, training, planning, mass media, social media, publications, manuals, coordination, conferences, motivation, collaborative projects, and joint action. All of this was directed toward the promotion of environmental sustainability, gender equality, socioeconomic justice, participatory governance, cultural tolerance, and peace and nonviolence. In this regard, I met with Courtney Bruch in Black Mountain and created a new Facebook page, "Compassionate Asheville."

In March through July, my focus was on completing my autobiography. In addition, I wrote a chapter on my spiritual journey for Joy Jink's next book, and endorsements for my former UNDP colleague, Dr. Nikhil Chandavarkar's two, brilliant historical novels.

In April, I participated once more in the ICA archives sojourn in Chicago, including giving a presentation on how the archives can be injected into the movement of movements. Colleagues Herman Greene, Nelson Stover, and Olive Ann Slotta also made early morning presentations. At the Archives meeting, the ICA Ukraine representative, Svitlana Salamatova, announced that her organization would prepare a Ukrainian language edition of my book. When it was ready, they want me to go to Ukraine to meet and speak with supporters of this cause. Other national ICAs were considering Hindi-, Chinese-, Spanish-, and Arabic-language editions. We also celebrated the completed life of our dear colleague Jean Long, the Archives Project coordinator. A surprise happened in the basement of the ICA GreenRise. While I was being shown around by colleague Ruth Gilbert, I reached into a random storage box and pulled out a book, opened it, and saw my mother's handwritten note inside, giving this gift to Mary and me for our first Christmas together in 1968.

On a hot May 17, I participated in a rally here in Asheville, supporting the presidential candidacy of Senator Bernie Sanders. In the general election, I will campaign for whomever is the Democratic Party candidate. The day of the rally was beautiful, and there were over 3,000 supporters gathered. I enjoyed being with other people of all backgrounds, ages, and walks of life who support environmental, economic, social, and political justice.

In June, I wrote in my journal: "Working on my autobiography has become a spiritual practice. I am discovering, and embracing who I am. I am learning to accept and celebrate who I am as I continue to evolve in compassion and understanding. It is a challenge to affirm who I am without being egotistical or narcissistic. I still have a big interior critic that says that I am insignificant, not smart, and a bad writer. I vow to retrain my inner critic to be my friend and cheer leader. Is it possible?"

Again in June I wrote: "Born on the cusp of the atomic cloud, a shy, Oklahoma small-town boy wakes up to his calling, studies

English and theology, joins the EI/ICA, travels around the world, lives in the villages of the world to be of help, then to the UN in New York City to advise cities and nations, witnessing the collapse of the twin towers, then to NYU to awaken and equip the minds and hearts of young public servants, finally becoming an author, activist and a grandpa at a time of climate chaos and ecocide."

On July 14 at 3 a.m., I went in to AFib again. I had been overly tired, writing until 10 p.m., had eaten spicy food late and too fast, got air in my stomach, had to stop eating and burp, and had a sugary dessert. Any of these can trigger AFib. I rested and stayed in AFib and rapid heartbeat all day. I wasn't able to be with the grandkids as planned. I experienced again that having a body was both a necessity and a big bother. The day was rapidly coming when I wouldn't have a body or an "I" anymore. I would be free to be part of mystery-love-gratitude forever and in myriad forms as "Ancient Treasure of the Heart" (my Buddhist name given to me by Drs. Larry and Peggy Rowe Ward.) After 66 hours, the longest time ever, I converted to a regular, slower heartbeat. I was so grateful and realized that I might live a while longer.

Also, I have been receiving helpful suggestions and affirmation from friends on social media related to possible titles and content of this autobiography.

On July 23, Grand Bonnie (her nickname as grandmother) and I took the grandkids to lunch at Troyers, an Amish place in Fairview, North Carolina, and to see a movie, *Toy Story 4*. It was sweet being with the two of them. Gratitude.

On the 24th, Bonnie's doctor told her that tests showed something concerning that needed further tests. I prayed that Bonnie would be OK and would live a long time.

The last week in this story

On July 25, Darlene Grooms and Carolyn Edwards came to Chickadee Cottage to help us make the place clean and nice. Bonnie and I met Myo, Aye, and Catherine Myint in Black Mountain at Thai Basil restaurant for lunch. They had flown from New York

City to Charlotte, North Carolina, and driven to Black Mountain. It was miraculous seeing them together after 14 years apart. They had said that they were coming to thank me in person for my role in helping resolve the visa issue that had kept them apart, but I assured them it was their own love and perseverance that did it. Later, I posted ads on social media for *A Compassionate Civilization*.

On July 26, Glenn Lamson came to Chickadee Cottage and made our flower garden shine. Bonnie and I took the Myints around Asheville, including to the Grove Park Inn, White Duck Taco (Myo's first taco ever), and the rooftop of the new AC Hotel for a panoramic view of city and mountains.

On July 27, I celebrated early my seventy-fifth birthday with family and friends at Chickadee Cottage in Swannanoa. After helping Bonnie prepare for the party, I took the Myint family to see the nearby Folk Arts Center. When we returned to my house, Bonnie, Jennifer, and Christopher set off a confetti shower welcome. Present were my loving wife, Bonnie, son Christopher, daughter-in-law Jennifer, grandson Phoenix, granddaughter Mariela, Kathy O'Neil, Jennifer's mother, and three friends from New York City, Myo, Aye, and Catherine Myint. My brother, Duncan, and sister-in-law Lisa, who usually attended my birthday celebrations were out of state. Son Benjamin was in New York; and recently married nephew Matthew Lindberg-Work and his wife, Kesha, were also out of state. I looked forward to a time when we could all be together.

It was a sunflower-theme party, symbolic of happiness, light, faith, loyalty, adoration, and longevity. Bonnie had arranged for sunflowers on the table, in the décor and wrapping, on the cake, and in the cards and gifts. We each read a sunflower quote. For example, "I want to be like a sunflower so even on the darkest days I will stand tall and find the light." "What sunshine is to flowers, smiles are to humanity." We celebrated my seventy-fifth year and the happy reunion of the Myint family. I read a poem

I had written for the occasion that began: "Seven and one half decades/ Long or short? A lot or a little?/ For a star, very short/ For a lizard, very long." The poem ended: "It is enough to live and/ to love/ Let's do it." We had delicious Nepali food and a vanilla birthday cake lovingly baked by Jennifer. My grandchildren made me beautiful cards, one with an Earth as the center of a sunflower, the inspiration of the cover of this book, and seventy-five colored circles, and the other with seventy-five candles. My wife gave me books of gorgeous sunflowers and a date at an upcoming French horn concert in Brevard, south of Asheville. Afterward, we drove to a nearby sunflower patch and took happy pictures. In this birthday celebration, I embodied and experienced gratitude and possibility for my life, family, friends, colleagues, and all people everywhere.

With Bonnie in our neighborhood sunflower patch

On July 28, Bonnie and I drove to Marshall, North Carolina, just north of Asheville, to meet Dr. Juliet Chieuw from the University of Aruba. Over coffee and cheesecake, she shared some of her experiences of the one-week women's retreat she had just completed. We also caught up on Aruba and new possibilities at the university.

On July 29, I continued working on my autobiography, completing the bibliography and sending out copies of the manuscript with requests to a few people to write endorsement blurbs. I confirmed with Jennifer that Bonnie and I would love to be with the grandkids Thursday morning while Jennifer took her mom to the eye doctor in nearby Hendersonville.

On July 30, I gratefully received yeses from the book endorsers— Shabbir Cheema, Martin Gilbraith, Lowie Rosales Kawasaki, Joy Jinks, Jan Sanders, Nancy Roof, Park Si Won, Jean Houston, and David Marshall. I worked on my autobiography manuscript and watched the Democratic Party debate in the evening. We each must do everything we can to change our political leadership and the direction of our country and world toward a compassionate, regenerative society.

The last day of this story

On my actual birthday July 31, the first thing I did after waking and visiting the little room was carry Mr. Chickabee, our fluffy, gray cat to the kitchen and fix his breakfast of wet and dry food. I then went to my study, checked my email and social media, and posted ads on social media for *A Compassionate Civilization.* Next, I sat on my floor cushion and meditated, being aware of each in breath and out breath. Following this, I stood before my altar, bowed, and chanted the bodhisattva vows to save all sentient beings. Then I returned to the kitchen and prepared my breakfast of yogurt, granola, blueberries, cranberries, walnuts, and almond milk. I received birthday greetings by text from my two sons and daughter-in-law. Christopher asked if we could have lunch together that day. My delicious, hot Bengal-spice tea was flavored with honey and vanilla soy creamer.

After enjoying breakfast, I took a hot shower, shaved, and dressed. Then I kissed Bonnie good morning and returned to my study to write and read. I took our garbage out to the roadside for pickup. I completed the manuscript of my autobiography, which you are reading! I hope that it engaged your imagination, sustained your interest, and was useful to your own journey of mystery-love-gratitude. I enjoyed an Indian lunch with Christopher. Bonnie and I picked up the grandchildren for a Chickadee Cottage sleepover. I went to bed, full of gratitude for this day and the accumulated gift of almost 39 million minutes or 234 million seconds of Earth-love since my birth. This is the last memory written here and thus completes the stories in the book ***Serving People & Planet: In Mystery, Love and Gratitude.*** May it serve!

Thank you, dear reader, for making this journey with me. I hope that it has been worth your while. May you realize peace, happiness, understanding, and compassion!

24

FUTURE SERVING PEOPLE & PLANET: Dreams, hopes, plans, eventualities - Swannanoa, NC

Author

As I dream, hope, and plan for any future moments, years, or decades that I may be given, I am working on a few other books and hope to publish several of them:

- *Thriving and Grieving during Chaos and Collapse*
- *Decentralizing Governance: Innovative Policy Perspectives*
- *Collection of Papers on Decentralization, Local Governance, and Innovative Leadership*
- *Power and Prosperity to the People*
- *Dancing Words: Selected Poems*
- *Ripples in Time: Selected Essays*
- *Innovative Leadership for Sustainable Development: Selected Speeches*
- *A Mystical Activist: Mary Elizabeth Avery Work*

The last seven titles have manuscripts in process. I may also write a memoir of my spiritual/philosophical/emotional reflections based on my 52 years of journals. More and more, I feel solidarity with every composite being, whether human, animal, plant, planet, or star. Each of us appeared from what had been before; we each lived our life; and we each transformed into what would follow. In this way I am like you. And you are like me. Together we are mystery-love-gratitude.

Activist

I also intend to continue my mindful climate/justice activism in Swannanoa, North Carolina, the USA, and the world to catalyze a compassionate-ecological civilization. I will work to get out the vote for candidates who care for people and planet in the primaries and in the general election in November 2020 and beyond. I will help the poor, the weak, the sick, the elderly, and the grieving. I will work with the Compassionate Asheville group, including offering Story Bridge, planning, and leadership training. I will help facilitate the work of the Compassionate Civilization Collaborative (C3) to strengthen the movement of movements (MOM) locally, nationally, and globally.

Because of climate chaos and ecological destruction, I will not fly, or very little. I hope to get an electric or hybrid car and use renewable energy in my home. Our yard should have a vegetable garden. I will not live near the shore of an ocean or a river that can flood. I will help myself and others grieve the death of many species and aspects of our civilization as we have known them and help my family and others respond to environmental and societal chaos and rebuilding. I will stay ever awake to new possibilities for life, creativity, and service.

Family, friends, and self

I will help my wife, two sons, two grandchildren, brother, sister-in-law, and other family members to be happy and healthy, and realize their full potential. I am daily committed to being supportive of Bonnie's health and happiness and her beautiful writing, publishing, and other initiatives. I want to share my deepest values with my grandchildren and help them discover why they are on this planet at this time. I will assist my friends and colleagues to achieve their life and work objectives. And with my colleagues who are approaching their own death or that of a loved one, I will enable them to make these journeys in trust, courage, kindness, and gratitude.

Mariela, their beloved Roo, and Phoenix: the future beckons

I plan to continue to care for the health of my body-mind, especially my heart, brain, eyesight, creativity, and attitude. I need cataract surgery and may need an ablation to help control my AFib. I will exercise daily and work out in the gym twice or thrice weekly. I will continue eating mostly vegetables and tofu or fish, drink plenty of water, and get enough sleep. I will meditate, pray, write in my journal, and read daily. And I want to be more compassionate with myself. Even though I am most often happy, I am sometimes unkind to myself and suffer from negative self-talk. May I be grateful for being the unique physical, mental, and emotional being that I am.

I would also like to play my French horn again, do some movement or dancing, and maybe do some acting in a local theater group.

At seventy-five, death is never far away. It could be in one second, one year, ten years, or twenty years. As is well-known, all beings and things pass away. This is the way it is in our cosmos and Earth. I will make death my friend and ask it to remind me of the preciousness of each moment of living. I will embrace my dying as an important part of my life. I am so profoundly grateful for the undeserved gift of my life.

Onward once again into mystery with love and gratitude!

EPILOGUE

In conclusion, I would like to share some temporal and thematic reflections on my life up to July 31, 2019.

Temporal reflections

Some of the high and low points of my seventy-five years of living and working are as follows:

A few of my joyful turning points:

1. 1965: Awakening in RS-1 to the fact and experience that I was accepted just as I am, and choosing to devote my life to helping each person in the world realize her or his full potential.
2. 1968: Marrying Mary Elizabeth Avery as my precious partner in creating a missional family within the EI/OE/ICA in service around the world to the least, the lost, and the last.
3. 1969: Traveling around the Earth in the Global Odyssey and falling in love with the Earth community.
4. 1974: Becoming the father of two precious sons, Benjamin and Christopher, while living and working with the ICA in South Korea.
5. 1990: Designing with Shabbir Cheema, launching at the Earth Summit, and coordinating the UNDP LIFE

program to improve the living conditions of low-income urban dwellers around the world.

6. 1992: Receiving a UN passport (*laissez passer*) as a symbol of being an international civil servant and a "global citizen."

7. 2005: Designing and implementing the UNDP DMIL program with Jean Houston and Jan Sanders to decentralize the MDGs through innovative leadership around the world.

8. 2007: Marrying Bonnie Myotai Treace as my precious partner in loving, grandparenting, teaching, writing, and saving all beings everywhere.

9. 2008/2010: Becoming the grandfather of Phoenix and Mariela to help them grow up as they help me grow old; and beginning to teach grad students from many countries at NYU Wagner.

10. 2013/2017: Writing a blog and publishing a book on *A Compassionate Civilization* to help reinvent society and save life on Earth.

Some of my sorrowful turning points:

1. 1960: Grieving the death of my precious Grandmother Work.

2. 1984: Grieving the death of my precious Grandmother Duncan.

3. 1995/2000: Shock and sadness at the discovery of my precious wife Mary's cancer and its return.

4. 1995: Shock and worry at my first episode of atrial fibrillation.

5. 2000: Grieving the death of my precious father.

6. 2001: Shock and sadness at 9/11, which shattered my sense of the world and began an era of perpetual warfare.

7. 2003: Grieving the death of my precious wife, Mary.

8. 2010: Grieving the death of my precious mother.

9. 2012: Sadness at the removal of my prostate through cancer surgery.
10. 2016: Shock and despair at the results of the US presidential election

Thematic reflections

In this next-to-last section, I would like to share a few aspects of my life and work and provide some overarching reflections.

"Be a useful man"

This was my Great-Aunt Mary's commendation when I was a boy. At university I woke up to my calling to "help all people realize their full potential" and I was a campus activist for women's rights, civil rights, and peace. I have been driven to serve during my entire life. I am an idealist in the sense of having a vision of what is needed and is possible; and at the same time, I am deeply practical in terms of being able to make things happen through detailed planning and implementation. I have always been a workaholic, and not just because my name is Work, although that may have helped. My favorite roles are those of group facilitator, adviser, trainer, coach and mentor, program and event designer, and writer, although I have also been a manager and a teacher.

Lover of the dance

I have always enjoyed dancing and watching dance performances around the world in different cultures. In university, I was too shy to try out for *West Side Story*, which I loved. Mary and I saw Nureyev and Fonteyn dance *Romeo and Juliet* with the Royal Ballet in Chicago soon after we were married. When I was 46, I fulfilled a lifelong dream and took ballet lessons at Purchase College conservatory for nine months. I loved it so much: bending, leaping, leotards, ballet slippers, turning, arms raised, bowing. I also enjoyed dancing at Jean Houston's Mystery Schools in New York. My UN retirement party was called the "Dance of Life" and included an ancient Greek group dance *Enos Mythos* and my solitary dancing to live guitar music of "I hope you dance." In my six-hour grad school classes, students did ethnic or popular group dances after every lunch. Why do I love dancing? Everything in life is in vibratory, rhythmic, and perpetual movement. There is only the Dance!

United Nations

In elementary school, I learned about the UN in our civics newspaper. I was touched by people of every nation who cared about the whole world and all its people and problems. Later in the Daily Office of the Order Ecumenical, prayers for the UN were in our liturgy, which we chanted every morning. When I returned to Jamaica to take part in a retreat, I had a strong sense and desire that being part of the UN was in my future. When I received my light blue UN passport (*laissez passer*), I was ecstatic that I was now officially an international civil servant (and citizen of planet Earth.) Since the time I was twenty-one, being a world server has been part of my identity, life, desire, and work. And if we didn't have the UN, we would need to invent it very quickly for the sake of dialogue, development, peace, and sustainability.

Reflective being

When I was a child, I loved looking at my thoughts and thinking about my action or inaction. What difference does it make to Sammy or me or his guests if I go to Sammy's birthday party or don't go? As a boy sitting in the barber chair, I had the experience of seeing my image repeated endlessly between the mirrors in front and behind me. I have always loved to draw and design things from my imagination. I have kept journals for fifty-two years, reflecting, planning, and reflecting again on my actions. I love the common sense and power of the ICA's ORID method of conversation: observing the objective aspects of something, reflecting on them, interpreting them, and deciding what to do next. I love

Joe Mathews's definition of the human being as consciousness of consciousness of consciousness. And I can never forget the words of Danish philosopher Soren Kierkegaard: "The self is a relationship that relates itself to itself, and in willing to be that relationship, grounds itself transparently in the power that posits it." Even though I love to be with people and to help other people, I must have time alone to think, write, recover, and regenerate my energy and direction. Even though I am not a professional philosopher, I think of myself as an everyday philosopher, brooding over the meaning and structure of experience and reality. I am also not a professional theologian, but I fancy myself as someone who is in love with mystery, spirit, compassion, and wisdom and wants to clarify what he understands and share it with others.

Earthling

When at twenty-four I first traveled around the Earth, I fell in love with her—her people, cultures, mountains, cities, villages, skies, and seas. Sunflowers make me happier than almost anything on Earth. I am a cat person. Skies, air, and clouds are my thing, much more than water or soil. Someone asked Father Pierre Teilhard de Chardin, "Why are you so happy?" He exclaimed, "Because the Earth is round!" Me too! Being a Leo, I worship all things solar, especially at Earth turn/sunset. Why am I so happy? Because the revolving Earth encircles our sun-star as together with all the planets we swing around the black hole at the center of our exquisite spiral galaxy, the Milky Way! My real reason: Life on Earth curves back on itself, thus creating one continuous surface; therefore, we will always meet, need, and help each other. I would rather build heaven on Earth than lift off to other planets that are not in the "Goldilocks zone," the perfect conditions for life. Gratitude for awe and fascination at being an Earthling. I have lived before the image of the round Earth for many years up to today – the photo is on my computer screen, two of my Facebook pages, the wall of my study, and the cover of this book. It was also on the wall of my UNDP office, at the front of my NYU classes, on all of my social media pages, on my name cards, and at Bonnie's and my wedding. Some call this whole Earth view the "overview" effect.

Family man

Family has always been very important for me. I have enjoyed being a son, grandson, brother, and cousin in my family of origin; starting my own family as a husband, father, and uncle; and then creating a new partnership (I love you, Bonnie!) and becoming a grandfather. Marriage itself may be one of the most challenging and rewarding spiritual practices of them all. I must confess, however, that my concentration and creativity have often been on my work throughout my life. I do hope that my attempt to be a responsible person in the world has not been a hindrance to my great love for my family. Somehow I have always tried to balance care for community, nation, and world, with care for family, and self.

French horn

Why do I so love to listen to French horn music, especially Mozart, Bach, Beethoven, Brahms, Schuman, and Strauss? Is it because I played the horn in high school and again as an adult? Is it the mellow tone and rich resonance? Is it the challenge of hitting the notes, especially in the upper register? Is it the beautiful, circular golden brass tubing and flaring bell? Is it the way you hold your hand in the bell to subdue the sound? Is it the way you create your embouchure that requires such tension and subtle flexibility of the lips? Is it playing and hearing the compositions themselves by such geniuses? Yes, it is all of those and more.

Spiritual journey

My spiritual journey began in Sunday school and Sunday services of the Christian Church. I was taught to love God and neighbor as myself. I then experienced an awakening of being accepted just as I am and a calling to enable others to realize their full potential in this life. I experienced transparent, demythologized Christianity, or secular profound humanness, that allowed me to understand the way life is (twli) and how to live what the Christian symbols were pointing to: that life is mystery, acceptance and possibility, freedom and obedience, and corporate care for others. I studied in graduate theological seminary. And I became a member of a secular-religious, family, ecumenical, experimental, global order that propelled me around the world in service to the least, the lost, and the last. Next, I experienced and loved the beauty and power of the Episcopal Mass. And finally, I came home to the profound philosophy and daily practice of meditation and study of Buddhism and vowed to be a bodhisattva and relieve the suffering of all sentient beings.

Sunflowers

Oh, yellow bright ones! How I love you. Your high stalks hold such perfections of small suns in perfect symmetry. You cheer me up. You greet me warmly. You always smile with nonchalance and dignity. You are our sun star growing up from Earth soil nourished by sun energy beaming down. You are yellow, yellow, and more yellow. In your center is such a large, round, pollen-laden labyrinth with worshipping bees buzzing, landing, nestling, flying away. You are summer and sunlight and the warmth of my birthday. Gratitude!

Language

Why do I love words, and grammar, and language? As a small child, I composed a long song and story in my native tongue, English. As a youth, I began to compose poems which I continued throughout my life. I studied Latin in high school and French in university. I majored in English language and literature in university, especially loving the American and English poets.

I spoke some Malay and Korean, and learned and spoke some Spanish in Venezuela. I have written so many articles, papers, chapters, speeches, and one other book. Language is magical and mystical and mysterious. How can a few marks on a page or a few sounds from the mouth give rise to such lofty thoughts, such full feelings, such energy and passion, such ambiguity or beauty? What are you really? How can this all work—the environment, the brain, the sense organs, conceptualization, imagery, sound, sight, giving rise to meaning, and emotion, and action, creating revolutions, and countries, and romance, and such grief-soaked word-sobs? A letter, a word, a sentence, a paragraph, a page, a book, and on and on until everything has been named, and commented on, and turned into . . . what?

Autobiography

Auto is self; bio is life; the life of the self. Writing this book has been a project, a spiritual exercise, and a retreat. I have been remade, remembered, recollected, refashioned, and reconnected. The thickness of my life was turned into words and finally into a book of paper and ink, my life as a book. I have cringed at my worst moments, my selfishness, my anger, my fury, my doubts. I have been made proud again of my accomplishments, creativity, risks, innovations, and service. This is part of my legacy, a leaving behind, a gift, a record, an accounting, a story to my heirs, to my race, to my Earth. But this life of the self contains only nonself elements—other people, things, events, and yet all me. It is a story of stories, a love story of my love of the Earth community and its love for me. It is my official and intimate report to people and planet. Why did I invest the time and energy to write and publish my life story in our moment of multiple crises? Couldn't I have been doing something more relevant to respond to these crises? My hope, my prayer is that my story and other such stories may encourage, inspire, strengthen, and equip those who are struggling and will struggle to recreate and care for human civilization and all species of life on Earth for eons to come.

Stories and meaning

One story of my life is that I began under an atomic cloud and am now facing melting glaciers. I have lived from the possibility of nuclear holocaust to the reality of climate chaos and ecological collapse. Yet the experience of my life has been that life is a gift as I attempted to be of service to people around the world. Another story is that I began as a shy, small-town boy and became a world server; what an unlikely story. Yet it is true; and it happened again and again by trusting the unknown, jumping into the abyss, watching for possibilities, and saying yes to some of them. Another story is that my work began with local projects, then shifted to national/global policies and programs, and then to awakening the minds and hearts of individuals. Or my work was first bottom up, then top down, and then inside out. Or the focus of my work was on community development, then decentralized governance, and then innovative leadership. Or I began in a small town in one country, then worked in fifty-five countries and served 193 countries around the planet, and then returned to a small town in my home country. Or I began in a small family of origin, then created my own missional family, then fell in love with the Earth-family, and finally returned to my small family. I love Joseph Mathews's wisdom that the meaning of life is not like icing on a cake. It is the cake. The meaning of your life is the life you lived. Buddhist wisdom is that there is no birth and no death. What could that mean? For me, it means that I was never aware of not existing and suddenly coming into existence. And I will never be aware of not existing. My only awareness is that of life, of being alive. There is only a continuous flow from the Big Bang to the present and onward. One of my favorite meaning stories about my life is that I really don't understand anything in this life except mystery, love, and gratitude. I have experienced life as bountiful gifts received and a few gifts given. I am grateful for being nurtured in a family of origin, creating a new family, and trying to be helpful to other families. I have experienced the love of the Earth community, and I have tried to love the Earth community. That is all.

Advice and recommendations

Be kind to everyone. Be courageous. Keep waking up. Trust the unknown again and again. Take risks. Stay true to your values and mission. Take care of your body, mind, heart, and spirit. Enable everyone to realize her/his gifts. Take special care of your relationships. Never stop working to make a better community, nation, and world. Protect other species and ecosystems. Keep discovering more of your own gifts and give them. Trust intuition *and* trust rationality. Work in four dimensions: changing mindsets, behaviors, cultures, and systems. Ask questions and listen carefully to the answers. Practice gratitude without end. Work with organizations that can act as your missional vehicles. Help others wake up and stay awake. Social and environmental development never end because things fall apart and need new efforts to right the wrongs and move forward. We live in the most critical time in human history; there is much to do; let's do it with urgency and commitment.

Blessings upon you!

POSTSCRIPT: YOUR REFLECTIONS ON THE BOOK

It might be worth spending some time thinking about and responding to the following four questions:

1. What do you remember from this book—stories, images, facts, feelings, people, events, things, insights, or ideas?

2. What emotions or memories of your own did you have while reading the book?

3. What did you learn about the meaning, significance, or lessons of this life story?

4. How might your life and work be different after reading this book?

Take some time, reflect, discuss with someone else, or write your thoughts. It could be useful. (This is the ORID conversation method of the ICA: Objective, Reflective, Interpretive, and Decisional.)

ACKNOWLEDGMENTS

There are many to whom I want to express gratitude for their transformative roles in my life and their help with this book:

Planetary ecosystems of water, air, soil, minerals, plants, and animals—thank you for your life sustaining, regenerative kinship.

People over the millennia who helped create languages, religions, cultures, and philosophies—thank you for these priceless gifts given to me and to many.

My parents, Rev. Moorman Robertson Work Sr. and Mary Elizabeth Duncan Work, my grandparents, and all my ancestors stretching back hundreds, thousands, millions, and billions of years—thank you for lives well lived and love generously given.

Doctors, farmers, and teachers—thank you for keeping us alive and educating us.

Rev. Vance Engleman and Rev. Joseph Wesley Mathews—thank you for daring to renew the Church in the twentieth century and inviting me and many to demonstrate the love of God around the world to the least, the lost, and the last through social, educational, and spiritual methods and models.

Dr. Jean Houston—thank you for inviting me to dance, to cry, to be more alive and creative in my social artistry.

Ken Wilber—thank you for developing an integral framework of transforming mindsets, behaviors, cultures, and systems which I use in my work.

Dr. G. Shabbir Cheema and Frank Hartvelt—thank you for believing in me and inviting me to be part of a global servant force for development and peace.

Dr. Paul Smoke—thank you for inviting me to share my methods, vision, and passion with graduate students from many lands.

Dr. Adriana Alberti, Dr. Shabbir Cheema, Joy Jinks, Dr. Jean Houston, Lowie Rosales, Dr. Tatwa Timsina, Rev. Dr. Mark Davies, Dr. Terry Bergdall, Karen Johnson, Jan Sanders, Jean Long, and others – thank you for inviting me to make keynotes, design and facilitate workshops, conduct leadership training, write papers, design curricula, and provide other services.

Gelek Rimpoche, and Drs. Larry and Peggy Rowe Ward—deep thanks for your teachings on the holy dharma of understanding suffering, impermanence, and interbeing and how to live a life of compassionate action, and giving me my Buddhist name "Ancient Treasure of the Heart."

Mary Elizabeth Avery Work—thank you for loving me and journeying with me for thirty-five years in service to people and planet.

Bonnie Myotai Treace—thank you for loving me these past twelve years, inviting me to be trustworthy and true, and providing your expert advice and kind support for this book

The many other family members and friends on and off social media who advised and encouraged me as I worked on this project, including Resa Alboher for recommending the book *Your Life Is a*

Book, Marjorie Bachert, Duncan Work, Catherine Whitney, and Jan Sanders for their suggested edits. Thanks also to editor Rob Mikulak, and to Lulu publishing.

And many, many more people and living beings.

APPENDICES

Appendix One: Author's online sites, publications, and other resources

Author's Online Resources:
A Compassionate Civilization (ACC):
    Amazon: https://www.amazon.com/dp/1546972617
    Blogsite: https://compassionatecivilization.blogspot.com/
    Facebook page:
    https://www.facebook.com/compassionatecivilization/

Movement of Movements (MOM) Facebook page: https://www.facebook.com/movementofmovementsMOM/

Robertson Work:
    Facebook page: https://www.facebook.com/robertson.work
    LinkedIn page: https://www.linkedin.com/in/robertsonwork/
    Twitter page: https://twitter.com/robertsonwork
    Amazon author's page: https://www.amazon.com/Robertson-Work/e/B075612GBF%3Fref=dbs_a_mng_rwt_scns_share

Videos of author's talks:
    Chicago. ICA USA International Dev. Think Tank Keynote. 2010:
    https://www.youtube.com/user/bergdall2
    Seoul. UN Forum Workshop Presentation. 2014:

https://www.youtube.com/watch?v=KQ3E1AZqFgw
Oklahoma City. OCU Peace Symposium Keynote. 2014:
https://vimeo.com/89274462
Fairfield, Iowa. World's Fairfield Peace Symposium Keynote.
2018:
https://www.youtube.com/watch?v=hSI5cHwS4TY&feature
=youtu.be
Colquitt, Georgia. Building Creative Communities Conference
Keynote. 2019: https://www.youtube.com/channel/UCf6RHm5
Hy-KT63DDsb9Ymlg/
Chicago. ICA USA Archives Collegium
Presentation. 2019: https://www.facebook.
com/icaukraine/videos/2833587292614 79/
UzpfSTEzNzI4NDg1NjU6MTAyMTg3Mzc1MzM0NT
QxMTM/

Podcasts of radio interviews with author:
North Carolina. *Thinking of Travel.* 2017: http://
speakingoftravel.net.buzzsprout.com/18461/603428-robertso
n-work-shares-how-to-become-a-global-local-citizen
Arizona. *Democratic Perspectives* #1. 2018: http://
verdevalleyindependentdemocrats.org/2018/01/17/
creating-more-compassionate-communities/
Arizona. *Democratic Perspectives* #2. 2018: http://
verdevalleyindependentdemocrats.org/2018/04/03/robertso
n-work-interview-podcast-april-2-2018/

Websites with author's interview, article, or book excerpt:
Buddhadoor website author interview. 2018: https://www.
buddhistdoor.net/features/creating-a-compassionate-civiliz
ation-an-interview-with-robertson-work
Garrison Institute website excerpt of ACC. 2017: https://www.
garrisoninstitute.org/blog/catalyzing-empathic-engaged
-citizens/

ICA International website excerpt of ACC. 2017: http://www.
ica-international.org/2017/08/14/compassionate-civilization-
urgency-sustainable-development-mindful-activism
-reflections-recommendations-rob-work/
American Buddhist Perspectives website excerpt of ACC. 2018:
https://www.patheos.com/blogs/americanbuddhist/2018/02/
burn-never-guide-compassionate-mindful-activism.html
Progressive Buddhism website excerpt of ACC. 2018:
https://progressivebuddhism.blogspot.com/2018/02/
how-can-we-build-coalitions-in-this.html
NYU Wagner website article on ACC. 2017: https://wagner.nyu.
edu/news/story/prof-robertson-work-out-book-compassiona
te-civilization-urgency-sustainable-development

Author's Publications:

Work, Robertson. 2017. *A Compassionate Civilization: The Urgency of Sustainable Development and Mindful Activism – Reflections and Recommendations.* Swannanoa NC: Compassionate Civilization Collaborative (C3).

_____. 2010. "Civil Society Innovations in Governance Leadership: International Demonstrations of Integral Development, the Technology of Participation (ToP), and Social Artistry". pages 112 – 130. *Engaging Civil Society: Emerging Trends in Democratic Governance.* editors Cheema, G. Shabbir, and Popovski, Vesselin. Tokyo: UN University Press.

_____. 2001. "Decentralization, Governance, and Sustainable Regional Development". pages 21 – 34. *New Regional Development Paradigms, Vol. 3, Decentralization, Governance, and the New Planning for Local-Level Development.* editors, Stohr, Walter B., et al. Westport CT: Greenwood Press.

_____. 2003. "Decentralizing Governance: Participation and Partnership in Service Delivery to the Poor". pages 195 – 218. *Reinventing Government for the Twenty-First Center: State Capacity in a Globalizing Society*. Editors. Rondinelli, Dennis A., and Cheema, G. Shabbir. Bloomfield CT: Kumarian Press.

_____. 2003. "Overview of Decentralization Worldwide: A Stepping Stone to Improved Governance and Human Development". pages 3 – 24. *Decentralization & Power Shift: An Imperative for Good Governance – A Sourcebook on Decentralization and Federalism Experiences, Vol. 11: Federalism: The Future of Decentralizing States*. Editors. Brillantes, Jr., Alex B, et al. Manila: Asian Resource Center for Decentralization/UNDP Philippines.

_____. Editor. 1997. *Participatory Local Governance: LIFE's Method and Experience 1992 – 1997*. New York: UNDP.

_____. Editor. 2005. *Pro-Poor Urban Governance: Lessons from LIFE 1992 – 2005*. New York: UNDP.

_____. 1998. "The Role of Development Assistance in the Area of Decentralization". pages 51 – 56. *International Symposium on Local Development and the Role of Government: New Perspectives on Development Assistance*. JICA. Tokyo: IIC/JICA

_____. 1995. "LIFE". pages 90 – 91. *Public Sector Management, Governance, and Sustainable Human Development*. MDGD/BPPS/UNDP. New York: UNDP.

_____. 2007. "The Global Citizen: A Love Story," pages 50 – 56, *Life Lessons for Loving the Way You Live: 7 Essential Ingredients for Finding Balance and Serenity*. Hawthorne, Jennifer Read. Deerfield Beach FL: Health Communications.

_____. 2009. "Strengthening Governance and Public Administration Capacities for Development: A UN ECOSOC Background Paper." New York: UN.

_____. 1993, *LIFE Mission Reports: Jamaica, Brazil, Pakistan, Thailand, Senegal, Tanzania, Egypt, Morocco.* New York: UNDP.

_____. 1994. *LIFE Report on the Global Advisory Committee and Donor Workshop, Stockholm: First Year Review and Strategic Planning.* New York: UNDP.

_____. 1995. *LIFE Report of the Second Annual Global Advisory Committee Workshop, Cairo: Phase 1 Assessment and Phase 2 Strategies.* New York: UNDP.

Author's Other Resources:
Fifty-two years of author's journals
Fifteen of author's photo albums
Sixteen years of author's UNDP staff review reports
Author's artifacts from around the world
Author's family letters and documents

Appendix Two: INTRODUCTION (1991, Caracas, Venezuela; and revised 1994, New York City, and 2019, Swannanoa, NC)

Getting a Running Start

Where to begin? I have wanted to write this story for how many years? It is a compulsion, a necessity. In order to move on, I must somehow muster my memory and creative powers to recall my years of existence and distill from this experience a body of knowledge, however small, which can be shared with other people.

At present I have only the depth intuition that there is something of worth in this effort. At present I experience a great unprocessed knowing that yearns to be processed and released like a laser into the stream of history. As so many others before me have done and so many after me will, I want to report on my contribution. My contribution to the historical process is called for as is every human beings. Once this is articulated perhaps I can move on to something else, something more, something as yet unknown.

In so doing I call upon the archetypes, the heroes, the counsel of wise beings, the angels, even God and whosoever, of whom I am not even aware, to be with me, to guide me, to release the well springs of knowing that I have known and know even now. It seems at the outset that this will take forever. I ask for strength, for steadfastness. I know that it is a finite task and that someday it will be completed in some form. Then I can move on. Then I will be released from this responsibility to tell my story so that it might be part of the larger story of my race, even of my planet, solar system, galaxy and universe – whatever that may come to mean in the distant future of the unfolding of evolution.

Where to begin? Fifty years ago? Five thousand years ago? Two million years ago? Four billion years ago? Thirteen billion years ago? Or today? What is the duration, the span of my story? This of course begs the question of, Who am I? Am I only this white, American, male? Or am I something more - something older, longer, more complex? Am I civilization? the human race? planet Earth? The universe become conscious of itself'?

Or am I merely this one who at this very moment is operating a word-processor, who yesterday was riding in a train, who in some tomorrow will die? Surely, in order to write this story I must circumscribe, delimit this "I" so that the story does not become the story of everything, which could become the story of nothing. And yet there is also this mysterious connection between the particular and the universal, between the eternal present and all-of-time, between the ego and culture, between this consciousness and Consciousness-Itself.

BIBLIOGRAPHY: BOOKS, AND ONLINE RESOURCES

Books and publications:

Bregman, Rutger. 2016. *Utopia for Realists: The Case for a Universal Basic Income, Open Borders, and a 15-Hour Workweek.* Amsterdam: The Correspondent.

Epps, John L. General Editor. 2005. *Bending History: Talks of Joseph Wesley Mathews.* Lutz: Resurgence Publishing.

_____. 2011. *Bending History: Talks of Joseph Wesley Mathews Vol. II Societal Reformulation – Toward a New Social Vehicle.* Lutz: Resurgence Publishing.

Mathews, James K. 2006. *Brother Joe: A 20ᵗʰ Century Apostle.* Lutz: Resurgence Publishing.

MDGD/UNDP. 1997. *Reconceptualizing Governance.* New York: UNDP.

Peterson, Brenda, and Freymann, Sarah Jane. 2014. *Your Life Is a Book.* Seattle: Sasquatch Books.

Griffith, Beret E. Editor. 2018. *A Chronological History of the Ecumenical Institute and the Institute of Cultural Affairs: 1952 – 1988.* Chicago: Institute of Cultural Affairs (ICA)

UNDESA. 2007. *Toward Participatory and Transparent Governance: Reinventing Government. DMIL/UNDP.* pages 74 – 82. "The Role of Civil Society Organizations in Localizing the MDGs." New York: UN.

UNDP. 1991. *Cities, People & Poverty: A UNDP Strategy Paper - Urban Development Cooperation for the 1990s.* New York: UNDP.

UNDP. 1996. *Urban Agriculture: Food, Jobs and Sustainable Cities, Publication Series for Habitat II, Vol. 1.* New York: UNDP.

Urban Development Program/UNDP. 1992. *The Urban Environment in Developing Countries.* New York: UNDP.

Online Resources:
East-West Center: https://www.eastwestcenter.org/
Global Archives of the Ecumenical Institute and Institute of Cultural Affairs: https://icaglobalarchives.org/
Institute of Cultural Affairs (ICA) International, www.ica-international.org
Institute of Cultural Affairs (ICA) USA: https://www.ica-usa.org/
International Association of Facilitators (IAF), www.iaf-world.org/site
New York University (NYU) Wagner Graduate School of Public Service, wagner.nyu.edu
Social Artistry, www.jeanhouston.org/Social-Artistry/social-artistry.html
Technology of Participation (ToP) Network, https://www.top-network.org/
UN Department of Economic and Social Affairs (UNDESA), www.un.org/development/desa/en
United Nations Development Program (UNDP), www.undp.org
UN Habitat, unhabitat.org

United Nations Millennium Development Goals (MDGs), https://www.un.org/millenniumgoals/

United Nations Sustainable Development Goals (SDGs), www.un.org/sustainabledevelopment/sustainable-development-goals

Universal Declaration of Human Rights, www.un.org/en/universal-declaration-human-rights/

ABOUT THE AUTHOR

Moorman Robertson Work Jr. is an author, ecosystem/justice activist, and founder of the Compassionate Civilization Collaborative (C3.) He has worked in 55 countries for 52 years and was United Nations Development Program (UNDP) principal policy adviser on decentralized governance, New York University (NYU) Wagner Graduate School of Public Service adjunct professor of innovative leadership, and Institute of Cultural Affairs (ICA) executive director in three countries conducting community, organizational, and leadership development initiatives. His undergraduate studies were at Oklahoma State University and his graduate studies were at Indiana University and Chicago Theological Seminary. He and his wife live in Swannanoa, North Carolina, near Asheville (Climate City), and close to family, friends, the Great Smoky Mountains, and the Blue Ridge Mountains.

He may be contacted at: robertsonwork100@gmail.com and would love to hear your reflections on this book, and on your life and work, your own questions and hopes, or your insights, requests, or advice.

Recent Book by Robertson Work

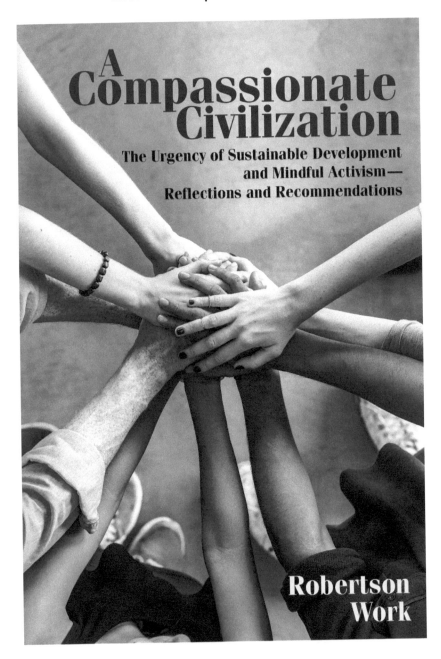